Magic In the Mess

*Unraveling the Lies I Told Myself to Discover
Who I've Been All Along*

Molly Booker

GATSBY
HOUSE
PUBLISHING

ISBN: 979-8-9913236-2-8 (ebook)

ISBN: 979-8-9913236-0-4 (paperback)

ISBN: 979-8-9913236-1-1 (hardcover)

For Kelly,

You are the magic in my mess, the melody in my chaos, and the love that has transformed my life. This book wouldn't be complete without acknowledging the extraordinary woman who has been my partner, my confidant, and my greatest source of inspiration.

Your unwavering support, boundless love, and belief in me have fueled every word on these pages. You've been the steady hand that guided me through the stormy seas of life, and the warm embrace that welcomed me home to myself.

In the messiness of life, you've shown me the beauty of imperfection, and in the quest for perfection, you've revealed the joy of being true to oneself. Together, we've discovered that true happiness resides not in the pursuit of external ideals, but in the acceptance and celebration of our authentic selves.

Kelly, you are my home, my heart, and my forever adventure. With you, every chapter of life is a story worth telling, and I can't wait to see where our journey takes us next.

With all my love,

Molly

Contents

Prologue

Bloody Mess

In the initial moments of waking, my brain conducted its routine scan: *Where am I? What day is it? What do I have to do today?* As I opened my eyes and took in the unfamiliar surroundings of stock paintings and stark-white walls in the darkness, I remembered: *I'm in Denver. I'm at the Comfort Inn. I'm here for the clergy retreat.* As I came to my senses, an unsettling sensation crept in. I felt wet. *Am I sweating? Am I having a hot flash?* Pulling back the covers, my heart raced as I discovered I was covered in blood. My clothes, the sheets, even the duvet were drenched. Panic, irritation, and anger surged through me. Despite the fact that this had been my new normal with my period for the past six months, the emotions felt raw.

The red 3:00 AM on the bedside clock glared at me as I disentangled myself from the bedding and headed to the bathroom for a shower. I scrubbed my clothes in the sink, rubbing them ferociously until my knuckles were raw. After tossing my underwear in the trash—they were too far gone—I threw on a T-shirt and jeans and hastily stripped the bed. Gathering the heavy linens into my arms, I headed to the hotel laundry room, hoping no one else would be there. As I shoved the heavy door open with my shoulder, I contemplated the irony of the moment. I had decided only months before that my New Year's resolution would be to "embrace the messiness of life," that my word of the year would be "mess," and here I was, scrambling to clean it up... again.

I took a mental picture of what was happening, my arms cradling piles of white laundry stained with red. It looked like a scene straight out of *Dexter*. *Fucking great,* I thought. *Just what I need, to turn heads by washing blood-soaked sheets at three o'clock in the morning at a Comfort Inn. Nothing comfortable about this inn, that's for sure.* I repeated the knuckle torture on the sheets, this time using abrasive laundry soap. Once I'd piled everything into the wash, I took a deep breath, set a timer on my phone, and went back to my room.

Now what? I wondered, sitting on the edge of my bare bed in the early morning darkness. I certainly couldn't go back to sleep without any bedding, even if I had been in a mental state conducive to rest. *Is this seriously happening?* I couldn't believe this was my life.

I ruminated over the bloody mess, spiraling about how it reflected my entire life. My marriage—my *second* marriage—was falling apart, less than a year in. I was a pastor. What would this mean for my job, for my relationships, for my ability to guide the congregation? Several of my longtime friends were dying of cancer, and my other friendships were failing. The world was trying to piece "normal" back together after a global pandemic, and I was navigating it right alongside everyone else. I felt like I was bleeding out emotionally, mentally, and socially, like life kept taking and taking with no reprieve in sight, no bandage to stop the bleeding. It was all building and building into an impossible mess.

Mess. The word reverberated through my mind and down my body, sending a queasy sensation to my stomach. It felt like spoiled food clawing its way back up, prompting my body to reject it. The visceral reaction confirmed that this was indeed my word of the year, and I couldn't escape it.

The day before, as part of the clergy retreat, I and several other pastors took the DiSC assessment, a personality test meant to improve our self-awareness and thus our pastoral skills. I was excited to take it; anything that unveiled insights about myself felt like a jackpot. As I tallied my results, my anticipation built. I felt like I was on a treasure hunt, about to unearth something precious, something invaluable. The final graph on the test resembled a large checkmark, and completing the test felt as satisfying as ticking off items on a to-do list. Flipping to the back of the provided packet, I found my profile pattern. The results, in three different areas, all pointed to the same conclusion: perfectionist, perfectionist, perfectionist.

This didn't come as a surprise, but it was still jarring. Reading the descriptions felt like I'd been put under an interrogation lamp: "Is restrained and cautious," "a goal of stability," "evaluates themselves and others by precise standards." It was as if a floodlight had exposed my innermost self. I felt simultaneously gratefully seen and uncomfortably exposed. Tears welled in my eyes before falling and splashing onto the paper packet in my hands. I had been running this perfectionist pattern since third grade, and realizing the toll it had taken made my soul feel weary. I craved stability and an end to ceaselessly trying to prove... what? Where was this relentless pursuit of perfection leading me, anyway?

I wiped my eyes with a finger as I stared defiantly at the results. The idea of being a perfectionist wasn't entirely negative; after all, it had earned me three master's degrees with honors. I prided myself on and defined myself by my achievements. *And yet*, I thought, *what would it mean to let go of this identity?*

There was a profound cost to this way of being. Perfectionism confined me to a tight box, often draining the life out of me. I reflected on my time in seminary, where I did the work for the grade and achieved good results but always felt a sense of tiredness and boredom. Grades felt like a matter of life and death, and anything less than perfect sent me spiraling. Playing it safe had become tiresome, and I yearned to push the limits, take risks, and not have everything figured out. What would it be like to emulate a "hot mess," swerving into the parking lot late (as always) and in a frenzy, opening the car door and tumbling out with my hair askew and weeks-old french fries stuck to my shoes? The allure of letting go, of loosening my hold on everything being just so, called to me, even as my eyes scanned the pages of my DiSC results.

Why had I always been so afraid to color outside the lines? As a child, I would get upset if the crayon strayed even slightly. I always painstakingly returned every single one to its proper place in the box in perfect rainbow order, and my two brothers' disregard for keeping them intact and sharp frustrated me. *How did I become wound so tight?*

The roots of my behavior had eluded me in those moments. Was I seeking stability? If I kept everything within the lines, would harmony prevail? My tolerance for conflict was minimal and being perfect seemed like the path to peace. Staring down at "perfectionism" on paper, I saw that peace for what it truly was: a self-imposed prison. I may have successfully reduced conflict in my life over the years, but it had robbed me of my freedom. Being alone in a peaceful jail cell was not freedom. There was a significant cost to this way of being, and while the results appeared favorable, if I turned the paper the right way, I could see that I was losing myself, drifting further from the fullest version of who I could be.

My timer chimed loudly in the early morning silence, pulling me out of my thoughts. I raced back downstairs, praying to God that no one would intercept my laundry. *What if the blood doesn't come out? What if someone finds out I bled the bed? What if someone discovers my mess?* In the moment, I thought that I'd rather be guilty of shitting the bed—at least I could blame a bad burrito or something. No matter how illogical it was, this felt like my fault. The bedding—my life—was a disastrous mess, and I had to clean it up before anybody saw just how horrible it was. I flung open the door to the laundry room, my heart thumping. It was empty. I wrenched the washer open and slumped in relief. The laundry was in, and soon, everything would come out clean.

After another round of timers and sneaking around barren hotel hallways like a criminal hiding evidence, I took all the laundry back upstairs and remade the bed. By the time I tucked in the last corner of the bedding, it was almost five o'clock; if I hadn't already been rushing around since three, it would've been time for me to get up. I was exhausted—another reminder of how I felt day after day, cleaning up one mess after another.

I showered, but less than two hours later, I could already feel the size five maxi pad reaching its maximum threshold. I went to change it and found it dripping, soaked tip to tip and through both wings. Blood had already leaked out, staining my new pair of underwear, too. I threw them away and cleaned myself up—again. The process of cleaning was mindless enough that it left me too much room to feel my feelings. For months, I'd been dealing with these insanely heavy periods, needing to race to the bathroom nearly every hour. I carried a "diaper bag" with me everywhere, filled with a huge bag of massive pads, extra underwear, and a Tide to Go Instant Stain Remover stick. I was so tired, and not just of the menstrual mess. I was physically drained. I felt exhausted all the time, and these tangible messes were just the tip of the iceberg. What was hidden underneath felt insurmountable.

I washed my hands and turned off the water with a squeaky

protest from the metal faucet. I grabbed the hand towel off the wall, and the enormity of the mess I'd created in my life, despite striving constantly for perfection, came crashing down on me. I sat on the bathroom floor, staring at the bloody underwear in the trashcan. I started crying so hard I began to choke and wheeze, unable to catch my breath. I lay down right there on the Comfort Inn bathroom floor. Was it even clean? I didn't care. My whole life was a fucking mess, so what did it matter?

Chapter 1

Good Girl

At the Comfort Inn, I couldn't make sense of my perfectionist tendencies. I couldn't fathom their origin, but I knew how they were hurting me, transforming messes into all-out disasters in my mind. As I reflect on my journey now, I see a thread weaving through the tapestry of my perfectionist life: the art of rule-following. Like an invisible force, the desire to please my parents and those around me had cast a spell, shaping the contours of my identity.

From a young age, I was taught the importance of adhering to societal norms, family expectations, and gender roles. Obedience and conformity became the currents through which I navigated my existence. At the time, it felt like simply following rules, but I've since realized it was so much more—it was about earning approval, love, and validation.

School was the first arena where I excelled at all these

expectations. The rules were clear, the expectations well-defined. I knew what I needed to do to get good grades, and I became great at doing just that. The acknowledgment and rewards for earning high marks became a template that I applied to all areas of my life, craving approval above all else.

But even from a young age, my struggle of navigating the dichotomy of staying in the lines and being true to myself was always present. My older brother, Ben, brilliantly modeled authentic self-expression and pushing the limits, and even though it was something I disliked about him, I also envied it. While he was very much his own person, pain seemed to follow him like a heavy cloud. He was moody most of the time, and I could feel the upset he created for people around him.

In high school, Ben got in trouble for illustrating a vocabulary word on a spelling test—one that meant "to spread widely" —with a woman spread-eagle. Listening to my mom's helpless voice and the teacher's horror on the other end during the phone call that followed, I felt simultaneously irritated that Ben had once again created upset and envious of the freedom with which he lived.

Ben constantly pressed up against people's comfort zones, and as a kid, I misinterpreted this as inflicting pain on them rather than him just being himself. I didn't like the way the world seemed to shift around him and the unpredictable nature of his moods. He embodied chaos, and it made me cringe. I didn't like not knowing what to expect from him. I wanted a well-defined path and clearly marked boundaries, so watching Ben as I grew up showed me how I could avoid rejection to earn love. I made up my mind in those early years without even realizing it: I was nothing like my brother and never would be. He represented chaos, uncertainty, and suffering. He was a mess, and I was determined to be different—the easy one, the good one, the smart one, the organized one. The good girl.

Those realizations became my foundation. I would stay in the lines, earn approval, follow rules, and please others. In exchange, I would have peace, acceptance, and happiness. People seemed happy with this arrangement. When I conformed, I got the love I needed, and that feedback was my inspiration to stay the course.

Even so, there were times I stuck my toe over the line in an effort to reach that ever-elusive, authentic part of me. I tested the waters from time to time, and *wow*, did it not go well. Once, in elementary school, I snuck into Ben's room, "borrowed" his camouflage Converse high-tops, and yanked them on with my favorite T-shirt and a pair of black pants. I rode all the way to school with a huge grin on my face, feeling like the king of the world as I navigated the hallways and classrooms. I could do anything in those shoes. Somehow, the world seemed brighter and full of possibility that day. The shoes were like my magic cape, granting me Ben-like superpowers to be myself. I strutted around school feeling like a million bucks. I just knew I was going to be the most popular kid in the building and win friends instantly with these things on.

I was so proud—until I wasn't. In the classroom, still basking in my awesomeness, I stood at my desk unloading my backpack as a few boys from the class noticed my shoes.

"Where'd ya get those?" one of them asked.

I knew it! I shrieked to myself. The boys were envious and wanted a pair. I was going to be a new trendsetter! But his next words decimated my confidence.

"Those are boys' shoes," he chided. I felt my cape disintegrate as my superpowers left my body.

"What are you, a boy?" another boy teased.

"Yeah, a boy—a *tom*boy," someone echoed. The teasing persisted, escalating into jokes about all my clothes and insisting I was gay. I didn't even know what a tomboy was or what "gay" meant, but I knew none of it meant anything good.

My stomach tightened and wouldn't release for decades. I'd hear the words of those boys the rest of the day, on the bus ride home, into middle school, and into adulthood. They repeated in my mind like a warped record that kept on skipping. I was equal parts confused and humiliated.

Why can't I wear those shoes? I wondered. *They are the coolest shoes I've ever seen! What's wrong with what I want to wear? Athletic pants with pockets are comfy and practical. Why are they calling me gay? What does that have to do with anything, and why is it such a bad thing?*

I wrestled with all of it for the rest of the day and came to the conclusion that there must be something severely wrong with me. What I liked was bad—so bad that if I embraced it, I would be ridiculed. What was the point of self-expression if it meant suffering?

Chapter 2

The Middle

Suffering wasn't just the result of trying to be myself in a world hostile to authenticity. I grew up in a strict household where disobeying the rules led to harsh punishment. Rule-following, whether the rules were unspoken or clearly laid out, proved over and over again to be the only way to avoid pain. Walking the line, the slim space between being fully myself and robotically following rules and norms, became imperative to me before I even realized I was doing it.

When I was 10 years old, my family gathered in the kitchen one morning in our home in Evergreen, Colorado. We were going about our normal activities, with Dad sitting in his chair at the head of the table near the fireplace and Mom was setting the table for breakfast. I sat still and quiet, making a deliberate effort to keep my elbows off the table. My brothers Ben (two years older) and Willy (two years younger) poked and prodded each other rowdily, nearly knocking a stack of plates out of Mom's hands. Still unruffled, she broke the news to us.

"Your dad and I are going out to dinner tonight with friends," she said. "We've called a babysit—"

Before Mom had the word "babysitter" completely out of her mouth, Ben, who was 13 at the time, immediately started complaining.

"Mom, we don't need a babysitter!" he shouted. "We're old enough to be on our own. What is she going to do that we can't?"

This type of arguing wasn't unusual from Ben; he argued about everything, always testing limits and pushing others' boundaries. He had earned the nickname "Wild Child" by always getting in trouble. His outburst made me unbelievably uncomfortable—another reminder that I didn't want to be anything like him.

Ben knew exactly how to push my mom's buttons just enough, and with a perfect sense of timing, to make her lose her temper. It was like he enjoyed watching her explode, which I never understood. She would yell, and it would all culminate in dishes being smashed to shards and scattered across the kitchen tile. Ben would be sent to his room—we all would—and that would be the end of it, unless my mom brought it up to my dad. He was the enforcer. His punishments were the opposite of my mom's. While she was loud and hot-tempered, my dad was cool, collected, and even cold at times. When he stopped talking and pursed his lips, we knew we were in for a spanking, a paddling, or the loss of some privilege. This scared all of us, including

Ben, but that didn't stop him from pushing—and despite his protests, the babysitter, April, showed up that evening.

"April is in charge," Dad instructed us with his jaw clenched and lips tight. "Whatever she says goes, and I mean *whatever* she says. Do you understand me?"

But it wasn't a question. His expression said it all—he had no tolerance for disrespect, and disobeying April would result in consequences. We could tell, both from past experience and the tone of his voice in the moment, that he would not tolerate anything short of us doing exactly what we were told. The instructions were clear. The path I needed to walk—the thin line down the middle—had been set.

As my parents pulled out of the driveway and away from our A-frame home, we looked forward to a night without the folks. I could see the relief on my brothers' faces as we watched them go, and I felt it, too. Growing up in the rural mountains of Colorado, we had no television, let alone any other electronics, and we were often bored. *Surely, April will be fun*, I thought. *She'll entertain us! Right?*

We turned away from the front door in anticipation. To our dismay, April opened her backpack, pulled out her homework, and sat down at the kitchen table without a word. In horror, I realized she was sitting in my dad's seat. No one sat in my dad's chair but him. We all had established spots at the table, and even if Dad wasn't there, no one else ever sat in that seat. It felt almost dangerous to see her sitting in his chair like it was her own. No one questioned my dad and got away with it. How did she make it look so easy?

Ben started in on April, calling her a bookworm and a nerd. Usually, this type of teasing was reserved for me, so I was delighted at the reprieve. Yet, April didn't react. I found it annoying that she was getting paid to ignore us. She eventually turned away from Ben, and that pissed me off even more. I usually found Ben irritating, but it was so rude to ignore someone when they were talking to you! That was one of the rules: You looked people in the eye when they were talking to you, and you responded. She'd been here all of two minutes and was already breaking all the rules. As my annoyance and resentment built, I felt myself slipping away from the line I was supposed to walk.

Suddenly, Willy, who was only eight years old, shouted in alarm. Startled, I looked over at him and saw blood pouring from his nose. This wasn't too concerning, as we often got bad bloody noses in the dry mountain air, but I wasn't going to miss an opportunity to make April do what she was being paid to do: take care of us. Ben and I both looked at each other knowingly.

"April!" Ben called out, pointing at Willy across the tiny kitchen. "Willy's nose is gushing—he's losing a lot of blood fast!" He was being a bit dramatic, which was further proof that he was just as annoyed at her as I was for ignoring us, but she didn't even look up. We couldn't believe it.

"April!" he yelled again.

Still nothing. Exasperated, we ushered Willy to the bathroom ourselves and eventually got the bleeding to stop, pinching the bridge of his nose and using a cold ice pack. All the while,

April sat at the table doing her homework like she was the only human in the house.

With the bleeding stopped, the three of us huddled in the living room and decided in hushed voices to go to the boys' room for a secret meeting. Willy followed up the stairs behind Ben and me, poking at the drying blood staining his green *Incredible Hulk* T-shirt. The boys were uncharacteristically quiet as they climbed the carpeted staircase. I kept my eyes fixed on my feet as we ascended past pictures of our family on the wall of the staircase. My dad had made the frames himself, and they felt like windows I was being watched through on my way to trouble, there to keep me from stepping out of line. Ben ushered us into his room and we gathered around his desk.

"April sucks!" he spouted. "She isn't doing anything, and she's wasting Mom and Dad's money. She didn't even look at Willy. We took better care of him than she did. She needs to go home!" For once, we all agreed. It felt good for it to be us against her instead of the usual us against each other. Quickly, Ben came up with a plan.

Ben had recently learned how to punch numbers into our landline phone to make it ring, and it was a new trick we were all quite proud of. We decided we would make the phone ring and pretend it was my parents calling to tell us they had changed their minds and April could go home. In our young brains, it sounded like a great plan.

As soon as the phone rang, April turned her head to the wall beside her to look at it, almost as if she were in slow motion. Willy and I sprang to attention while Ben rushed into the kitchen and over to the phone, picking up the receiver with a flourish.

"Hello, Booker residence, this is Ben speaking," he said in a practiced tone. We were instructed to always answer the phone this way, and even in this situation, we didn't dare stray from the rules. "Oh, hi, Mom. Yes, everything is good and—what's that? Oh, you changed your mind and we don't need a babysitter anymore? Oh, okay. I'll tell April and send her home."

I worried that April would see right through the pretend phone call and we'd end up in huge trouble, because Ben was being a bit too obvious. It didn't sound like a normal conversation—it sounded like Ben pretending to hear exactly what he wanted. Even so, it seemed to be working, because April was listening intently. Ben hung up and told April my mom had changed her mind and that she could go home. Without a word, April gathered up her books and walked out the door. She didn't even say goodbye.

We ran to the front door and peered out the tiny window squares, each of our faces pressed up against a small pane of glass as we watched her walk down the driveway and out of sight. We all turned and looked at each other before screaming and jumping up and down. *Victory!* I was so proud of Ben in that moment for looking out for me and Willy. We were a team. No one messed with the Booker kids.

For the rest of the evening, we got along great. We worked together to make ourselves dinner, cleaned up, did the dishes, and straightened up the house. We did all our chores so everything would be in order when my parents arrived. I expected them to be proud of us—we had taken care of Willy, saved them money, and cleaned up after ourselves. We had done everything just right: we had followed all the rules.

When my parents came home, Dad scanned the kitchen. "Where's April?" he demanded. The energy immediately changed in the room, and you could hear a pin drop as we all went silent. Just moments before, I had been full of pride at how we'd handled ourselves while our parents were away. But now, his severe tone was a dead giveaway: he was pissed. Ben was the first to speak up.

"She went home," he said quietly. My dad demanded an explanation. We had learned long ago never to lie to him, so we confessed that we had tricked April. My dad was as mad as I had ever seen him, and without a word, he left the house. He told us later that he drove over to April's, paid her, and apologized to her and her family. When he got home, he sat us all down at the table and took his seat by the fireplace.

"What you did was unacceptable," he said. "You put April in a horrible situation, and you embarrassed all of us." I felt a lump in my throat. We had embarrassed my dad, and that was the worst sin of all.

My dad was silent for what felt like forever. We all sat there with our backs straight and arms by our sides—no rowdiness and certainly no elbows on the table. In the adjoining living room space, my mom sat on the couch and didn't say a word; she never did once Dad had taken charge. No one argued with Captain Bob Booker, United Airlines pilot and resolute father.

After what felt like forever, Dad told us to write April an

apology letter, explaining that its quality and sincerity would determine the extent of our punishment. I felt so baffled. Why were *we* in trouble? April had left without even talking to us or checking with our parents. Ben's plan had been awfully weak, and yet she had still left us, just like that. She hadn't even tried to help Willy when he had a nosebleed—and she sat in Dad's chair! Why didn't *she* have to take any accountability?

We wrote the letter, which I thought was incredible. We were polite and honestly apologetic, owning that we'd put her in a bad position and acknowledging how we must've made her feel because of what we'd done. Yet, the letter wasn't good enough for my dad. He was so unimpressed that he instructed us to go down to the basement and make a paddle, which he would then use to spank us. My heart dropped. The paddle was the worst, and it stung so badly. I could still remember the searing sting of the wood against my bare butt the last time we had been made to do this, and the embarrassment and shame of bending over with my pants down.

I wasn't sure what time it was, but it was well past our bedtime as the boys and I went outside to the basement access, descended into the unfinished room, and turned on the flickering light. We cut a paddle out of wood and made a separate handle. Ben connected the handle to the paddle with only a single nail, hoping it would make the paddle a bit weaker so my dad couldn't hit us as hard. It seemed like a good idea.

We took our paddle up the stairs, into the dark, back into the house, and finally into the living room, where we lined up somberly. Ben was always first, then me, and then Willy.

When my dad wound up and smacked Ben with the paddle, the handle broke off. Dad was so furious that he cussed—a very rare thing. He picked up the paddle again and spanked Ben so hard it made him cry. It was one of the rare times I saw my older brother in tears, and I was terrified to go next.

When Dad had finished with Ben, it was my turn. I bent over and hoped maybe my dad would go a little lighter on me, since I was the girl—but the first hit came so hard and so fast that it took the wind out of me. After that, they kept on coming: *Whack! Whack! Whack! Whack!* It was excruciating. When it was over, I struggled to catch my breath, and when I finally did, the tears came. Dad hadn't even started in on Willy yet, he he had already started to cry.

I don't know what was worse, getting paddled myself or hearing the wood hit my little brother's behind. I think I cried harder when it was his turn. He tried to be tough, bar barely letting out a whimper as his tears fell silently with every whack. I knew it was taking everything he had not to let out even a peep.

he was doing everything he could not to let out a peep. My heart was broken. Not only had I helped Ben come up with the plan, but I'd helped him go through with it. Stepping out of line hadn't just gotten me in trouble. Everybody had suffered for it. When it was all over, the three of us ran upstairs, got right into bed, and cried ourselves to sleep. My butt was sore for a long time, although I never said another word about it. None of us did.

Chapter 3

Special

More than the spankings, I dreaded disappointing my dad. He would purse his lips and go quiet, which I dreaded more than anything. I could feel the anger and frustration in his silence like a knife cutting to my core. I felt indescribably separate from him in those moments. More than anything, I wanted to be special to him, for him to be proud of me and approve of my choices. I thought if I copied what he liked and mirrored him, I could earn his love. I leaned into all the things he loved—school, math, science, airplanes, and running.

I thought that if I liked what he liked, it would make me lovable. The disastrous flaw in this belief seems obvious now, but I didn't realize then how damaging it was. I didn't feel good enough just as I was. There was something wrong with what I liked to wear, what I loved to do, and the things I said. I lost confidence in myself and developed an understanding that everything I liked, believed, and felt was worth less than the likes, beliefs, and feelings of others. I began to turn outward for validation rather than trusting my own truths. Abandoning myself and my own sense of knowing, I began copying others, especially Dad, to avoid rejection. Over time, I started to forget I was doing it. It just happened as though I was on autopilot, and my authentic self became less and less accessible until I didn't know where others ended and I began.

When I was in fourth grade, my dad made a deal with me, Ben, and Willy: "If you get straight As, I will take you on a trip anywhere you want to go in the US." I knew it was a challenge he had designed for Ben and Willy rather than for me. I always got good grades, but neither of my brothers cared about school nearly as much as I did. I could see right through his plan, but that wasn't going to stop me from taking advantage of it. Dad wanted straight As, and I'd get them for him. If there was a bar set or a prize on the horizon, I was all over it, and this was no exception. In a rare showing of courage, I went up to my teacher, Mrs. Morris, and asked her what I would need to do to get all As. She didn't say I had to do anything too differently,

I don't remember her saying I needed to do much differently, but she took the request seriously. I could see on her face that she knew how important it was to me. Even for me, getting perfect marks would be challenging. We were graded on everything from PE, art, and music to handwriting, math, and behavior. There must've been nearly 30 grades every semester to keep up with! It felt nearly impossible to be perfect at them all. I'd gotten close many times before that, but that year, after my dad had issued me a specific challenge, I did it. My little achiever brain danced in delight as I raced my report card home to my dad. I was going to get my special trip!

I chose San Diego specifically to visit Sea World. We went for three days, just me and my dad, and when we got there, I was mesmerized by the sea life, the water, the cool blue colors, and Shamu. That first morning, while Dad was out for a run, I rubbed my feet back and forth beneath the starched hotel sheets. We didn't have a television in our house; Dad always said it was better for us to spend our time on other things like playing outside, reading, or doing homework. Sleepovers were a welcome treat, because we could binge TV on Saturday mornings and eat sugary cereal.

Since Ben had been diagnosed with Type I diabetes when he was young, we never kept sugar in our household—it was strictly Cheerios or Wheaties for us. But on that first morning in San Diego, I delighted in watching morning cartoons in bed. I snuggled in and ate dry Lucky Charms from the free breakfast in the hotel lobby, like popcorn from a Styrofoam bowl.

I relished the pastel marshmallows in my cereal, the cartoons flashing on the TV, and the bed, with sheets that were so white and soft. I felt the smoothness on my little legs as I pulled the covers up to my neck, immersing myself in the magical bedding. Everything about it felt special. This was it: I had finally earned a reward. It was more than a treat for me. It was heaven.

As a middle child and my parents' only daughter, I often

felt left out. Ben was always causing trouble and required a lot of attention due to his diabetes. Willy was the golden baby of the family, and everything seemed to come easy to him—he excelled at sports, making friends, everything. He had charisma, and everyone adored him (including me, as much as I hated to admit it).

I felt so ordinary and in the middle with my talents as a bookworm and student. Even so, I knew school and learning were important to my dad, who had a PhD in electrical engineering, and so they were important to me, too, even if my brothers teased me, calling me a nerd and a brownnoser. I knew they were right, but what else did I have? School was my thing—and look where it had finally gotten me!

Just when I thought the trip couldn't get any better, my dad came in the door all sweaty from his run and told me I had a choice to make. *What?* I thought. *I get to decide something? This is new.*

"On my run, I found another hotel down the street that is a bit cheaper," he said. "It's not quite as nice, but if we move over to that hotel, we could stay an extra day. Your choice."

He looked at me expectantly as if I'd need a minute to process. I didn't. Of course I wanted to stay longer! The other hotel could've been a one-star garbage dump, and I'd still want to go there if it meant extending our trip. In the end, switching hotels allowed us another day, which meant going to the San Diego Zoo! The trip just kept getting better and better, and it was all thanks to my perfectionism.

Following my accomplishment in fourth grade, the expectation to get perfect marks was locked in. I knew this would please my dad, and even before he suggested a trip and some special time with him was suggested as a reward, I was all about it.

For the rest of my school career, I was obsessed with my marks. I received only two Bs all throughout high school—the rest were As. Those two Bs came the semester after a traumatic event rocked my family, and even with that understandable strain, I didn't let myself off the hook.

I adored my dad and held him as the golden standard. He was brilliant, he was a pilot, he ran marathons, and he fixed everything around our house. He was the one in charge, the one with money and power. If we wanted something, we had to ask him. Even my mom asked his permission for things. He ruled the household, and I was envious of his influence. I wanted to be a pilot, just like him. I wanted to do *everything* just like him.

My mom, on the other hand, seemed so weak to me. She was stuck doing all the boring, unenjoyable chores. She made our clothes, sewed, cleaned, did laundry, made our food from scratch, and even ran her own business selling portable, pop-up kids' playpens called Turtle Tents, which I found kind of dumb. Very few people wanted one at the time and she struggled to get traction (though they're everywhere now).

As a kid, I considered anything my dad did cool and anything my mom did lame. She was the glue in our family, but I didn't see her strength. I thought women were weak, and I wanted to push all my femininity aside as a result. I didn't want anything to do with cooking, cleaning, laundry, or anything "girly." Men had the influence and the power. *Dad* had the influence and power. So, if I could be like him, maybe I could have those things, too.

Despite all that, I loved my mom and we always had a good relationship, but it wasn't until my forties that I began to see my mom's real strength and power. Growing up, I certainly held a skewed view of her and of women in general. The patriarchal way my family operated was evident among us kids, too, not just Mom and Dad. The standard was different, and this pissed me off. Even though he was younger than me, Willy could stay home alone; meanwhile, I needed a babysitter, even in high school. My dad would offer my brothers a sip of his beer, but never me. He would let my brothers go camping together but refuse to let me join them. I couldn't be with the boys.

This skewed view of men versus women was just more motivation for me to prove that I was enough, especially to Dad. I wanted to be *special* to him more than anything. I wanted him to be proud of me, and his pride was something I thought I could earn. Sea World was *special*, and I had earned it. *Surely*, I thought, *I can do the same with the other things I desire?* Just like that, it was locked in: being special was something you had to earn.

I became a master at earning Dad's approval and feeling like I was special to him. I knew I could outwork just about everyone at school, and I did, despite the sacrifices and effort required. While I earned more trips than we could take through my school career, something debilitating was happening without me knowing it. That striving and those rewards were creating a belief system; I began to believe that earning and achieving equated specialness and worth. Effort and perfection weren't just expectations, they were requirements.

My nickname as a kid was "Wheels", because I was so fast on the soccer field, but it fit for other reasons I couldn't see at the time. Inherent in my system of earned worth was the required belief that I wasn't worthy on my own, that worth was outside of myself. As hard as I worked, as much effort as I put in, as often as I succeeded, it was never enough. The carrot—or, in my case, the sugary cereal—was always just out of reach. Like a hamster on a wheel, I ran my heart out with no end in sight. Sometimes, I still catch myself on that wheel, running my heart out; the irony of it all is not lost on me.

It never occurred to me that special time with my dad was a right, not a privilege. It touches deep to articulate that. I always thought his love was something to earn. This misunderstanding nearly cost me my life in suicidal depression years later. I've learned a lot about worth, specialness, and love since then.

Chapter 4

Between

Adolescence, with its tumultuous waves of self-discovery, often serves as a time for rebellion, a period when individuals carve out their unique identities. For me, however, rebellion was an alien concept. My fear of disappointing my parents by deviating from their prescribed path led me to tread cautiously, tiptoeing through the labyrinth of others' expectations. Ever since the camo Converse incident, I knew deep down it wasn't okay to do anything that wasn't "normal."

As I grew up, I saw Ben as proof of this. I witnessed him spiral into depression and enter a world of drugs and alcohol. I misunderstood his pain and thought his authentic nature created this suffering for him, much like wearing those shoes had for me. Watching Ben struggle reinforced my belief in following the path and not pushing boundaries. Not doing it was making my brother eat himself alive. Clearly, it was dangerous out there.

The space for authentic self-expression seemed more and more elusive, overshadowed by the weight of conformity. I became a proficient tightrope walker, balancing on the thin line between the person I was expected to be and the person I was. The art of camouflage became second nature—masking my true feelings, desires, and identity under layers of societal expectations. I did all my homework, did my chores, chose my clothes from the girls' section, and said "yes, ma'am" and "no, sir." I was an easy kid. I prided myself on this.

Being a rule-follower brought a peculiar sense of comfort. It felt like a protective shield guarding me against the uncertainties and potential disapproval that awaited beyond the boundaries of convention. I got a hint of this rejection any time I leaned into my masculine side as a kid. That day I wore Ben's shoes wasn't the only time other kids were relentless in teasing me, calling me gay and a tomboy. I hated the ridicule and shied away from further rejection. Little did I know that this shield would eventually become the very obstacle hindering my journey to self-discovery.

As the years unfolded, the walls of my carefully constructed fortress grew higher. My fear of disappointing my parents, especially my conservative father, held me captive within the confines of a life that wasn't authentically mine. It wasn't that I didn't harbor inklings of my true self. I had just become adept at tucking them away, deep within the recesses of my being. I felt my truth wasn't good enough, and there was always something wrong with it: I shouldn't want to wear boys' clothes. I shouldn't like my hair short; cutting it made me ugly and unattractive; I should love skiing, hiking, and running just like the rest of my family.

I constantly felt like a gender failure, and somehow, what I liked always felt wrong—like I was taking happiness away from others. I thought if I didn't like skiing, it would take away from the love my family had for the sport. So, I hated it and did it anyway. I forced myself to do what I thought others wanted and tucked away any internal strife it caused me. Doing so eroded my self-trust and hid my knowing under many false layers.

The weight of others' expectations was a silent burden I carried for years, and it made it challenging to discern where the rules ended and my true self began. Every step away from the prescribed path felt like a betrayal, not just to my family but to the version of myself that had dutifully followed the script for so long. The irony lay in the fact that the very rules meant to guide me obscured the most critical rule of all—know thyself.

I vividly recall the first time I sensed the constraints of gender expression closing in on me well before the Converse shoes. I was no older than five when Ben and I were out on a hike with Dad—one of many moments of exploration and adventure. I cherished these times, eagerly anticipating the surprises nature had in store for us. Our journey began as soon as we stepped out of house and onto a nearby hiking path, which was situated on a steep hill. The path, though well-trodden, was rocky and narrow, allowing just enough space for one person. The rugged terrain didn't bother me; it felt like paradise.

Under the sun's warmth, a few hundred steps into our hike, Ben rocked my world. "Molly needs to put her shirt on," he commanded. Neither he nor Dad had shirts on. My confusion was palpable. Dad swiftly dismissed Ben's demand, but the unspoken tension lingered. I could sense a hidden truth, something Ben knew that I didn't, something Dad wanted to shield me from. I continued walking shirtless, but my mind was spinning. What was wrong with me? Why was it okay for Dad to be shirtless but not me? This marked the genesis of my lifelong struggle with gender expression and conformity, a persistent feeling that I was missing something or that something was inherently wrong with me.

In fifth grade, I encountered similar confusion in less well-known company. In elementary school, I cycled through a series of best friends. My best friend at the time, Maggie, had decided to host a mixed-gender party for her birthday that year. The anticipation left me uneasy. Maggie's excitement to plan such an event only heightened my sense of dread. I couldn't fathom why I felt this way, or why Maggie wanted such a party and I didn't. My anxiety reached its peak as we set up for the event. The unfamiliarity of it, coupled with the pressure to conform, made me retreat to Maggie's room, desperately wishing my mom would pick me up. Maggie was so enthusiastic, but I was filled with dread.

To get to her basement, we descended the stairs from the living room, but the energy struck me as strange. I'd been there before, but as we prepped for the party, the whole place felt unfamiliar. *Something's changed*, I realized. For the first time, we weren't decorating the space with things we loved and thought were awesome—instead, we were preparing with the boys in mind.

"What color do you think they'll like?" Maggie asked me, holding up a bag filled with streamers, balloons, and other party trappings. She wanted everything to look good for them, and her desire to please the boys made my stomach turn. I didn't feel the same way and, once again, the thought crept in that I was a gender failure. I had to hide my confusion and disgust. My feelings about the party were messy—I feared they could cause me to lose friends and the tiny shreds of social status I clung to.

As we waited for everyone to arrive, Maggie introduced me to the concept of "the licorice game." In the middle of the basement, there was a table with a plastic cover on it where she had arranged an assortment of chips and soda cans. Maggie brought out these really long strings of red licorice and carefully arranged them on the table. As Maggie explained the game to me, miming how the opposite ends of the licorice strings went into a boy and girl's mouth, I struggled to concentrate. The contrast between my love for Maggie, her house, and her family with this *boy* thing was like a chasm. It was like there was a cost to the happiness and joy that came with her friendship—a price I couldn't, or wouldn't, pay.

Once everyone arrived and settled in, spin-the-bottle loomed. I hung back, but Matt, the popular boy, urged me to join the circle. I felt torn. I was thrilled at the attention yet terrified by the prospect of kissing a boy. The internal conflict left me paralyzed, and the crowd's chants added to my embarrassment. Instead of rescuing me, even my closest friends questioned, "Are you a prude?" It felt like drowning while the rescue boat doused me with waves. The message was clear: saying no was unacceptable. Social acceptance required embracing romantic involvement with boys.

That year began a strange dynamic between me and the boys at school. Boys who once valued my athleticism now distanced themselves as romantic relationships took precedence. My tomboy image, once celebrated, now isolated me. This culminated in the first boy's attempt to court me—a pattern that repeated, which led me to reject others' advances and intensifed my desperation for acceptance.

As time went on, I became torn between not wanting a boyfriend and feeling the need to belong. So, eventually, I somehow convinced myself that I needed to find a relationship. My desire for a boyfriend became an urgent need, linked to my self-worth and social status. I was now searching, desperate to find someone who would date me. Every rejection deepened my fear of being unlovable and undesirable. The fear of lifelong loneliness haunted my nights, leaving me feeling like a defective product with no return policy. I was stuck with this body, this mind, and the situation seemed utterly hopeless.

When the last year of elementary school rolled around, Bobby came along. He asked me out through one of my friends and, to my horror, I froze. I didn't even give myself a chance to think about it; I just panicked and said a resounding, "No."

My friend pushed back. "Why not? He's a great guy and he really likes you," she insisted.

Well, I hadn't given it much thought. At a gut level, it almost felt like I'd given up, but why, I didn't know. The truth was I didn't have a reason. So, doubting myself and without any good excuse for my friend, I acquiesced, and I was going out with Bobby.

Several timesm he tried to say hi to me in the hall, and I choked. I couldn't utter a single sound, and I began to ignore him. This whole thing was turning my stomach into knots. *Why can't we just go back to the way it was before and all be friends? Why do we have to go out with each other? What does that even mean?* After a few weeks, Bobby got tired of me ignoring him and broke up with me. I felt immense pains of rejection, and even that made no sense. I didn't even like Bobby, but I felt like a loser. He broke up with me. He didn't want me, which was an assault on my worth.

I became obsessed with Bobby, with solving this puzzle. How could I "do" gender right? My failure with Bobby made me push harder to figure it out and to fit in.

For the next several months, I could only think about Bobby and how he had rejected me. I wanted a boyfriend, but I didn't. I wanted Bobby, in a way—but in my heart, I didn't. I struggled to make sense of any of it.

As junior high approached, my hope dwindled further. My lack of a boyfriend morphed into a broader absence of friends. Even my sanctuary, soccer, where my athleticism was celebrated, failed to bridge the gap between my on-field and off-field identity. The rejection of my tomboyishness in school left scars, leading me to quit soccer, sacrificing the one place where I felt truly accepted. I often found myself eating lunch alone—a searing experience that made me physically ill.

Back in elementary school, we exchanged $1.25 for a tray of a meat, vegetables, bread, and milk. We had to sit with our class, so finding a spot by someone to talk to felt easy. The only choice we were given was whether or not we wanted chocolate milk for an extra nickel. Now, in junior high, we got to choose what we wanted: fries, pizza, chips, or even candy. I loved having the freedom to choose junk food, but even that couldn't make the lunchtime experience bearable. As my eyes scanned the cafeteria, I could hear the heavy plodding of my sneakers on the cold linoleum floor slow, like I was wading through water. I panicked, wondering where to go. The other kids had formed friendship groups around the fold-out tables, and even though there were plenty of empty, round seats, none of them felt accessible. It was like staring at the promised land but being unable to go in.

Jumping in or inviting myself to a table felt impossible. I scanned the room, desperate to spot a familiar face but always unable to. Every day, I'd walk into the lunchroom, excited to fill up on pizza and candy and ready to relax—and then, within minutes, I'd have a stomach ache as stress tightened my insides into knots. The rejection felt like a force field that the whole cafeteria seemed to be screaming at me. It was the one place I couldn't hide.

After finding no one to sit with, I would throw my lunch

away and head to the library. I told myself I wasn't hungry and that I wanted to go and read, but I was really devastated. Of course, I wanted to laugh, joke, eat junk food, and share my fries with someone. The pain of loneliness and rejection was so intense that I buried it in books—I couldn't let myself feel how badly I wanted these things.

My isolation fueled a deep desire to vanish, which, tragically, would eventually morph into a wish to no longer exist.

Maybe this will stop after junior high, I hoped. *Maybe everyone is feeling this way and high school will turn it all around.* I couldn't wait for the nightmare I was living to be over.

As I waited out the summer before high school, the registration packet finally arrived in the mail. My heart raced as I stood in our dirt driveway, cradling the box with Evergreen High School logo on its side. *Yes!* This was it, my ticket back to my happy life. Things were starting to look up.

My older brother Ben had returned from rehab as a new person. He was no longer cold, mean, angry, and addicted. He was the older brother I thought I'd lost long ago. Now that I was about to start at Evergreen, for the first time in a long time, we would be at the same school again. I would be so proud to show up there with him. This was going to be good.

As I tore open the package, my eyes scanned the registration instructions and flew from page to page until they suddenly stopped. My heart felt like it had frozen in my chest; my stomach tightened. I reread the sentence over and over. Each student was to come to registration and line up with their locker partner. I didn't have one. I felt panic consume me. I *had* to have a partner for this to be different. I couldn't start high school as my loser, junior-high self, even if I did have Ben there for moral support.

There were four people I could think of that I occasionally said hi to in the halls in junior high. I felt nervous in every part of my body calling them, but this was life or death. I had to make this happen. Each person informed me they already had a partner. It was devastating: I was starting high school without a locker partner.

Fortunately, the horror of showing up single didn't last long, because I found someone in line who also didn't have a partner. I felt like I'd been thrown a life raft just as I was drowning. It didn't matter to me that we weren't friends; it just mattered that I wasn't without a person to line up with. Yet, the damage to my sense of self was already done. It was official: I was a loser. I wasn't good; I wasn't lovable. What had gone wrong? How had I become so ugly, stupid, and worthless? I felt like everyone around me had the instructions to this thing called life, and I was trying to play without them. I felt so lost and alone that the pain became almost unbearable.

Six months in, things hadn't improved much, but thankfully, I did have one friend—someone who I studied with and ate lunch with: Elizabeth. This was a huge improvement from junior high. We quickly found each other in our advanced classes, because we were the two nerdiest people in the class. I think we both appreciated our mutual desire to do well in school and genuine love of learning. We would sit, legs crossed, in the hall between classes and share equations, excitedly pointing at our TI-85 graphing calculators and marveling at all they could do.

Elizabeth provided solace, but our deep connection invited teasing, including being labelled gay. My confusion deepened. Why was I being singled out? Why did this keep happening to me? The pressure to conform intensified, and my need to find a boyfriend to secure a sense of belonging resurfaced.

I never really understood my relationship with Elizabeth. We seemed to connect on school, learning, and nerding out over things, but there was always a distance between us. It was like we were best friends, but we never talked about anything other than school. It was confusing to me. I wanted to be closer to her, but there was something in the way. We didn't hang out together on weekends, and I didn't know how to open up to her.

What little progress I had made on reclaiming my worth during high school vanished that January. Ben was killed in a car accident on his way home from school. He had asked me the night before to go with him to get his truck fixed. I had said no— one of the only times I'd stood up to him—and he died because of it. It was my fault.

I was no longer just a loser; I was a murderer. My *being* hurt people. That was my new truth: my being alive caused everyone around me unbearable pain. The best thing for me to do would be to cease to exist. For everyone's sake, the most loving thing I could do would be to disappear, to die. This became my wish. I wished that I would stop waking up in the morning. Then, I wished I would get in a car accident, fall to my death, some- thing. I wished for the courage to slit my wrists—I even tried it a few times, only to fail at that as well. I was the worst. I hated myself and longed to die.

Suicidal ideation and occasional attempts became my secret and my shame. I thought about dying all the time, and with each thought, the shame festered. I was ashamed that I wanted to kill myself, that I was secretly the reason my brother was dead. I couldn't eat. I couldn't sleep. I couldn't focus. I had almost no friends.

Elizabeth and I still sat next to each other in class and ate lunch together, but we never talked about my brother. We shared the same space at school, but we never connected in any meaningful way. I was desperate for connection, but I didn't feel I could ever get it. At the same time, I clung to the threads of our friendship, trying to keep it alive and terrified that I'd find myself in the same position I was in during junior high of having to eat alone.

Everything was wrong with me. I wasn't anything like the other girls in school who were obsessed with makeup, clothes, and boys. I couldn't care less about any of that. I liked wearing boys' clothes and loved to read and study. Despite having no interest in boys, I still desperately wanted their approval if it would get me out of this nightmare. *That has to be my ticket out,* I reasoned. *I can be fixed by someone who loves me and feels that I'm was special.* This was my solution, and I was determined to fight for my entire life to find it.

High school was a continuation of this painful narrative: The rejection, questioning of my identity, and desperate desire to belong lingered, and my internal conflict persisted. I was caught between a reluctance to embrace romantic involvement with boys and the societal pressure to conform. This clash intensified my feelings of being defective, undesirable, and fundamentally wrong.

When I got to college, I thought things could be different. I just needed a fresh start. I traveled all the way to the coast of Maine from the mountains of Colorado for a pre-orientation trip before my first semester of college. I wanted to get as far away from my reputation as possible, and the coast of Maine seemed like it might be far enough. When I arrived, I was horrified to realize I was on an all-girls trip and most of them were gay! I'd never even met a gay person before then. How was I ever going to get a boyfriend now? As the years passed, I grew more ashamed and more desperate. I wanted more than anything to have a boyfriend so people wouldn't see my ugliness and unlovability, but the harder I tried, the worse I felt. The more I tried to clean up the confusion of my life, the messier it got.

One night during my first year of college, I was standing against the wall at a fraternity party with some of the other girls from my rugby team. Boys weren't on my mind at that time, as I'd resigned myself to the reality that I was undesirable. As the party continued, I sipped my drink and watched my fellow classmates float around the room. A group of boys walking in the front door caught my eye. Everyone turned to stare at them, instantly aware that they were strangers. Our town was small enough that folks from out of town were easily recognizable. Word traveled as fast as fire around the room that they were from a nearby military school. They were all fairly muscular and in great shape. I admired their strength, authority, and the way they commanded the room, but I felt jealous at how they effortlessly sauntered into the party and engaged in conversation.

The frat house always smelled a bit like beer and pee. The floor was sticky from spilled beer, and the wooden picnic tables in the dining area were perpetually covered in empty beer cups and residue. I kept my arms tucked in and stood away from the tables and walls, too disgusted to risk touching anything.

One of the boys from the military school helped himself to a beer and approached me. Was this it? After nearly ten years of desperately wanting a boyfriend, was it finally going to happen? I couldn't believe my luck.

He introduced himself as Steve and struck up a conversation with me, occasionally pausing to offer me sips of his beer. He was so nice! Sharing his beer with me and letting me drink out of his cup felt so intimate. He was adamant I keep drinking. In my excitement and desperation, it never occurred to me that he was trying to get me drunk. It wasn't until we were in the woods, with him holding onto my hand too tightly, that the sinking feeling came over me. By then, it was too late. This "boyfriend" would take my virginity by forcing himself inside of me.

I thought this was what I wanted. I thought I was desperate to lose my virginity, to kiss a boy, to hold hands, and to have sex, so I wouldn't be unlovable. I had gotten my wish. This boy had done all those things. It was my first kiss, my first time holding hands, and my first time having sex. But it wasn't sex; it was rape, and I did not feel lovable. The experience made me feel worse than I ever had before. He used me and then threw me away, literally leaving me lying in the dirt like his discarded beer cup. I felt disgusting, foolish, and ugly. Here was more proof that something was wrong with me, more evidence that I was unlovable.

I numbed the pain with alcohol and work. I studied constantly and ended up graduating with honors from one of the toughest colleges in the country. I went on to push my way through three master's degrees. Working, striving, and getting things perfect became my most effective way to quieting my internal voices of shame and disgust. I thought that if I just tried a little harder, if I earned just a little more, if I was good enough, then maybe I could outrun my shame and my unworthiness, maybe I could hide under layers and layers of success and accomplishments.

These experiences, imprinted in my formative years, cast a long, dark shadow. The fear of being undesirable and forever alone became my constant companion. The internalized belief that my style and expression were wrong and unattractive fueled a debilitating, suicidal depression. I was losing myself in my desperate attempts to fit into a mold that I never truly belonged in.

Chapter 5

Direction

Eventually the time came for me to apply for college, and I chose Bowdoin College in Brunswick, Maine. I wanted to get away from Colorado—go far, far away —and Maine felt like a good option. The son of a man who worked at the same ski area as my mom in Colorado went there, and he told me it was an easy party school. On top of that, the name sounded cool and mysterious, so I was convinced. I was elated when my application was accepted.

In my first semester of college, it became immediately obvious that the other student had misled me—Bowdoin College turned out to be academically rigorous, and I was forced into the deep end with almost constant tests and mountains of reading.

I went home to Colorado for Christmas break and met a guy

named Jason, who worked at one of the local ski shops. He loved dogs, and he was into hiking, kayaking, and the outdoors. He seemed nice enough, and I thought a quick week-or-two fling would be the extent of it. I was shocked when, just after New Year's, he asked if we could continue to date long-distance when I returned to school. I was floored! After years of striving, it was finally happening. This would be my first real boyfriend, and *he* was the one who wanted it to continue. I couldn't believe my luck!

We dated for the rest of my junior year and decided to spend the summer together at Rocky Mountain National Park. He had gotten a job as a park ranger, and this afforded us the ability to actually live in the park, a rare privilege. We jumped at the opportunity, and I quickly found a job at one of the campgrounds, managing reservations. The office where I worked was in the same building as our apartment! I could literally roll out of bed and be at work. It was amazing. I felt like I was really living the dream.

One afternoon, Jason needed to do an overnight at one of the cabins in the park, and we decided it would be fun if I met him there after I was done with my shift. I was a bit nervous about getting to the cabin by myself, but I'd been there before and felt equal parts scared and excited at the challenge of making it happen. All day, I'd been running through the steps in my mind and was determined to get them right. I pictured myself walking up to the cabin and him greeting me with a huge hug. We'd have dinner, snuggle in the cabin, and have a great night in the wilderness. We'd get up early, make a fantastic breakfast, hike back together, and still have the entire weekend ahead of us. I knew it was going to be great.

Sitting at my desk, I glanced up at the clock for the hundredth time that afternoon: 3:14 p.m., only two minutes had passed since the last time I checked. I went through it all in my head again, also for the hundredth time. I would leave work at 4:30 and quickly change out of work clothes into the hiking clothes I'd already laid out. I would grab my water bottle out of the refrigerator, gather my overnight hiking pack I'd loaded the day before, and be ready to go. I'd just need to turn off all the lights, lock the door, and drive over to the trailhead a few miles away. I calculated that I could be on the trail hiking by five o'clock, and I'd make good time up to the cabin to meet Jason. I had thought everything through and planned painstakingly.

Finally, at 4:15, I couldn't stand it any longer. No one was around, and the office had been dead all afternoon. I decided to close up a few minutes early. I shut off the lights in the office and hung up the "Closed" sign, along with directions on how to sign in to the campsites after hours. I smiled with satisfaction at the tidy, organized office space, knowing I had left it in pristine condition.

I headed into the apartment, up two simple steps from the office, and scanned the room. Everything looked spotless. I fluffed a couple couch pillows for good measure, but I had already cleaned the place during my lunch break. Still, it couldn't hurt to just check one more time to make sure everything was in order. I grabbed my water bottle and fit it into the side pocket of my hiking pack. I groaned as I hoisted it onto my back and wriggled it on my shoulders to settle its weight. As I headed toward the door, I realized: I didn't have my keys! *Whew*, I thought. *At least I remembered before I got to the car, otherwise I would've wasted precious minutes.* Jason and I were sharing the Subaru for the summer, and I always left the keys on the counter right by the door—but they weren't there. I didn't even know where else to look.

Ugh, why didn't I think of this sooner? I chided myself as I set down my pack and began pulling open kitchen drawers. Not there. I checked Jason's jacket pockets. Nothing. *Shit.* I checked the bathroom, the bedroom, and the kitchen again. Still nothing. I went back into the office to make sure I hadn't set them down in there for some strange reason. Not there either. I emptied my entire pack and rummaged through the pile of extra socks, granola bars, flashlights, and other hiking essentials. No keys.

I checked the clock. It was 4:45 p.m. I felt my heart begin to race. All that extra time I'd gained by clocking out early was dwindling before my eyes. In desperation, I retraced all my steps and looked in all the same places. By five o'clock, I had searched everywhere twice. Nothing. I stopped and took a deep breath. I had no idea where the keys were, and I realized during that breath that every minute I kept looking for them put me further and further behind. I could just walk to the trailhead. It would only add two miles to my hike, and the extra time spent walking would still be less than what it would take me to find the keys. I could do this.

With my heart still racing and my anxiety clouding my thoughts, I heaved the pack back onto my shoulders, turned off the light, locked the door, and headed out. As I walked, I began calculating in my head. *If I jog to the trailhead,* I thought, *I can make up a little time.*

I jogged the two miles to the entrance to the trail, replaying the timeline in my mind over and over. How behind was I compared to when I had planned to arrive at the cabin? How fast would I need to go to get there when Jason was expecting me? Even though it was impossible, I ruminated on wanting to be early. Barely on time would have to do, and even that was possible only if I hustled.

When I arrived at the trailhead, I started to relax. I tried to slow my breathing and drop my shoulders, letting the weight of the pack pull them down. It had taken me 26 minutes to cover the two miles. *Not bad,* I thought. My original plan was to be at the trailhead by five, and it was 5:26 when I arrived. If I pushed myself and didn't stop for breaks, I could close that twenty-six-minute gap. Buoyed by the possibility of being on time, I walked briskly up the trail, constantly checking my watch, calculating my mileage, and smiling when I realized I was gaining ground. Occasionally, my pace would slow, and I would grumble in frustration. Very much like watching the GPS while driving and trying to beat the estimated time of arrival, I obsessed over my calculations and progress.

I have no idea what I saw on the trail; I was so preoccupied with getting to the cabin, I completely tuned out the journey. Maybe I saw wildlife, beautiful flowers, or ancient trees? I wouldn't know. I had my eyes trained on my feet, willing them to go faster, and on my watch, willing time to slow down.

When the trail veered to the left, I realized something felt off. I had been on this trail before and knew it should be leading me off to the right. Despite the uneasy feeling in my belly, I couldn't slow down or stop to double check. That would make me lose precious minutes. I kept on going, trying to convince myself that this was the right way and I was on track.

The objection in my gut grew with every step I took. I started to doubt myself. I oscillated between slowing down to heed my uncertainty. The clock was ticking, so I had to choose wisely. This had to be right. I couldn't afford it not to be.

I nearly bumped into the sign before I noticed it. Though the trail was not going the way my intuition was screaming for me to go, the names on the sign sounded right, so I convinced myself to keep going. I even picked up the pace.

When I turned a corner and saw the campground, my entire body went tense. Suddenly, I could see what I'd been trying to ignore for the last few hours. The reason the signs sounded familiar was because they were leading me to Jason's ranger station, not the cabin! I had been walking completely in the wrong direction for hours! I was supposed to be at the cabin right now, and I had just hiked at least three miles the wrong way. I wasn't anywhere near where I was supposed to be. How had I messed this up so badly?Reality began to settle in: I was lost. I didn't have a map or any way to get in touch with anyone, the ranger station was empty and locked, and I wasn't anywhere near where I needed to be.

I thought back to all the wilderness survival courses I had taken and the Hug-a-Tree classes I'd attended as a kid. Like most Colorado kids, I was required to take them in elementary school. They were run by a nonprofit that taught kids if they got lost in the wilderness not to run or panic; instead, they should hug a tree and stay put. You weren't supposed to keep walking, as you would usually end up going in the wrong direction and exhausting yourself. This had been true so far. I had known something wasn't right but kept going anyway, as fast as I could —and in the wrong direction.

I looked around. I was in a clearing near a campsite. Off the trail, there was a picnic table. I scurried over to it, took off my pack, and rested it on the table, taking in my surroundings. I could hear the evening bugs and birds starting their songs as the light faded in the distance. It was just starting to get dark. My shoulders and the back of my shirt were soaked with sweat, and I became frustratingly aware of the temperature dropping.

I sat down and took a breath. *Okay, Molly, be smart here.* I reached into my pack and grabbed an apple. I needed to get some food in my system and to think logically about my next move. My brain told me to run back down the trail to try to make up for lost time, but something in me told me to stop—to take care of myself and really think before rushing off. I then had a glimmer of realization: If I had slowed down and listened to my intuition in the first place, I wouldn't be in such a mess. But it faded as quickly as it came. I had to get *where* I was supposed to be *when* I was supposed to be there. It took every- thing I had not to start running. I sat and ate the apple in silence, my anxiety growing with the darkness. I couldn't believe I had messed up this badly. Jason was going to be so mad. Past experiences with his short temper and bullying made me certain of that.

I told myself that people would start looking for me soon. Jason was a park ranger and had a radio he could use to talk to all the other park rangers. He would send word that his girl-friend was missing, but that thought sent panic coursing through me instead of comforting me. This was so embarrassing, and Jason was going to be furious. I was more worried about his reaction than the fact that it was getting dark and I was now about six miles or so from the cabin. I either had hours of hiking in front of me, or I could settle here for the night and hope to be found the next morning.

I reasoned that the best thing to do would be to get on the correct trail. In my hurry, I had missed a turn somewhere and ended up on the wrong one, where no one would know to look for me. I finished my apple, changed my shirt, put on a fleece beanie, and fastened my headlight on my head. Then, I secured my pack and started hiking again before my anxiety gave way to more calculations. The next three miles would be downhill—I could make up some time. Once again, the clock in my head started ticking.

When I reached the correct trail, it was fully dark, and while my headlight pierced the darkness directly in front of me, it didn't go much further than that. I could feel panic pushing in on me. I imagined coyotes, bears, and mountain lions with every crunching leaf and falling twig. *It's just a squirrel*, I repeated at every sound I heard. *We are okay,* I said into the darkness like a mantra.

As I stepped onto the correct trail and started the trek back to the cabin, I realized I would probably come across someone looking for me at any moment, which still only brought embarrassment instead of relief. *I was foolish to miss the turn, to fail at to doing something so simple,* I thought, feeling shame settle in. *How did I let this happen? I'm better than this.*

I committed to continuing up the correct trail rather than stopping to wait for someone to find me. I'd meet anyone who was out looking for me eventually, and every step I took would bring me closer to where I was supposed to be—closer to *less* foolish, *less* shameful. I picked up my pace and the miles began to drift behind me. My calculations forgotten, I now had thoughts for only one thing: making progress to minimize my shame and embarrassment. *Just get closer to the cabin,* I kept thinking. *Close the gap between where you are and where you should be. You're not where you should be. Close the gap.*

It was just after 9 p.m. when I saw the lights of the cabin glowing ahead of me and finally felt a wave of relief. I had made it all the way there without being intercepted—never mind the fact that I was safe and no longer lost and alone in a national park. What was most important is that I had gotten back on track before I was caught.

The cabin stood like a beacon before me, a physical representation of my success. As I approached, the door flung open and Jason came running out. He emerged from the hut still wearing his full ranger uniform with his hat and snug-fitting shirt, stained with mustard. Had he been eating while I was lost? I could imagine him sitting there, casually enjoying a sandwich while I was panicking, trying to find my way in the darkness. I still couldn't help but smile. I'd finally get a hug and a warm greeting, maybe even praise for surviving the trek. I'd made it.

"Where the hell have you been?" he screamed at me as my mind struggled to catch up. *Shouldn't he be relieved and excited to see me?* "Do you know how worried I've been? What the hell is going on?"

My mind scrambled to take in that he was mad—furious, even. I couldn't talk, couldn't even choke out one word. Tears pooled in my eyes as all the adrenaline of the afternoon and evening caught up to me. I started crying and managed to gasp, "I got lost." But it didn't matter what I'd gone through. What was important was the discomfort I had created for Jason. I'd worried him. I'd upset him.

He told me that he'd freaked out at the thought of needing to put a call in to the other rangers that I was missing. That would have humiliated him. My mind began to process what he was saying: he never reported me missing. I was over three hours late, and he hadn't called anyone. Alarm bells were going off inside me that something was all wrong here. *He should be comforting me, not condemning me,* I thought. *Right?*

Just like the voice on the trail that tried to tell me I was heading in the wrong direction, I ignored the thought. I shut the voice down and decided quickly that I had to make up for my mistake. I hustled inside, dropped my pack by the door, and hurried into the kitchen to make dinner. I could do this. I could make up for everything. I could salvage things and ensure Jason wouldn't break up with me over my stupid mistake. I could repair the damage and ensure he never realized just how unlovable I was.

Chapter 6

Choke

Twenty years later, I still hadn't cured my self-recrimination or gotten rid of all the calculations still zipping around in my brain. The measuring continued, along with the constant calibrating and stifling my inner knowing. I constantly felt pushed in directions I somehow knew were wrong, but I stayed on the path anyway. I was a good girl, after all.

My relationship with Jason had long-since ended, and with one failed marriage in the rearview, I was living in a home that my first husband and I bought together—a townhouse in Eagle, Colorado that was perfect in just about every way. We had finished the basement to include a bedroom, a sleeping and reading nook, a bathroom, a TV area, and even a sauna. I had hand-picked every piece of furniture and paint swatch, and the result was a modern, clean space that felt like a luxury hotel.

I loved it there, but I rarely allowed myself to use its many features because I was too afraid of messing them up. I wanted to keep everything nice. The upstairs included the primary bedroom, a guest room, and a room I used as an office. It was a lot of space for just me, but it felt perfect. Everything was just as I liked it: clean and organized, with everything in its place.

One afternoon, I reached into the refrigerator and grabbed two grapefruit soda waters, my favorite. I picked up the cold cans and placed one on my forehead and one on my neck, enjoying how refreshing they felt.

"Ah," I murmured, allowing myself a few seconds to enjoy the cool metal on my skin. After a moment, I snapped my eyes back open. It was time to double-check that I had everything for my overnight stay at Stagecoach Reservoir, and I needed to take my new puppy, three-month-old Otis, out for a final pee. I needed to get moving.

I put the cans in the cooler with an icepack and a few apples and set it by the door with everything else I'd need for the weekend. I had packed all of Otis's things first and was surprised how much stuff a small puppy needed. I had food and water, poop bags, a few toys, his leash, his soft crate, his bowls, and his therapeutic bolster dog bed—nothing but the best for my baby boy. I had carefully packed my bag as well with swim gear for standup paddling, fun shorts and T-shirts for hanging out by the lake, a few cute things to sleep in, and a few dressier things for dinner in Steamboat. I scanned the pile again. Bug spray? Check. Sunscreen, both face and body? Check, check. Hat and sunglasses? Check and check.

I picked up Otis and gave him a squeeze. His droopy, Boxer face wiggled in my hands as he licked my cheek, which melted my heart. He could tell we were heading out for something, and his little stub of a tail was wiggling so hard his entire backside was moving. I felt a sense of ease and excitement. Everything was falling into place. I had gotten up early that morning at five o'clock sharp and cleaned the house, which always felt like a must before I went anywhere. Cleaning the house, emptying the trash, and clearing out the refrigerator before leaving for an overnight trip felt as essential as putting on my seatbelt before pulling out of the driveway. My obsessive cleaning that morning finally gave me the jolt of peace I so craved. For a few minutes, my mind relaxed, and I felt good about myself.

I grabbed Otis's leash, smiling with the satisfaction of having checked off all the boxes. We headed out to the small park in the center of the townhome complex where all the other local dog people and I gathered in the mornings to drink our coffee or tea together and watch the dogs go at it. Otis and I headed toward the grass with him straining to get there, ready to pounce on his friends, his butt still wiggling excitedly until we sat on the wet grass.

I inhaled the brisk air, fifty degrees of rejuvenation against my face. My old Denver Broncos hoodie felt like a security blanket around me. It had molded to the shape of me after so much use, and even though it was worn and thin, its familiarity provided all the warmth I needed. I smiled as I unclipped Otis and watched him bound toward his friends. The sun was just coming out. I thought about the weekend ahead and felt a giddy rush of nerves as I delighted in how everything was coming together.

I had a weekend date—an overnight date with an amazing guy I'd known for years named Eric. I had a feeling this was the start of something great. This single life, this dating nightmare, was about to be over. I just knew it.

I'd met the last guy I dated online, but he had ended up being a pathological liar. We met online. His lies were all over the place, from benign to outrageous. He had beamed with pride as he told me about cleaning up body parts after the Challenger explosion; he'd been the only coroner on hand at the time, he'd explained. Once, he claimed that he had completed an ultra-ultra-triathlon, complete with a 100-mile swim—but it didn't stop there. He also said he'd swum inside a cage towed by a boat during it, so he'd be protected from sharks.

Ultra-ultra-triathlon? One hundred miles? *Sharks?* I was a pretty trusting person, but he had constantly been stretching even my sense of plausibility. He also ended up stealing my electric bike and $5,000 from me. I was so embarrassed and humiliated. Fortunately, I had caught on and broken up with him before he could do any more damage.

After involving the police and getting about half of my money back, we broke up, and I swore off online dating. I had been such a fool, and I was determined not to allow anything like that to happen again. The clock was ticking, I was closing in on 40 fast, and I still had dreams of being a mom. Years before, I thought I'd already been about to check those boxes off just in time. A few months before my 30th birthday, my internal deadline, I had gotten married to a man named Tom—but after seven years together, it was clear our marriage wasn't going to go the distance.

Tom was 23 years older than me, and we were best friends. He took care of me in every way, and that had felt more suffocating than helpful. I felt like such a brat. *Oh, poor me, my husband takes care of me too much. He does whatever I want and won't stop asking what he can get me or what I need.* But I felt crippled in that relationship. I wanted more. I wanted passion. I wanted disagreement and excitement. I wanted to feel alive. My first marriage was so flat, so safe, and so perfect. As it turned out, sometimes things could be *too* perfect.

This confused me, because I had been chasing perfection my entire life. I wanted someone who could help me check all the boxes off, and Tom had been a master at it. We never ran out of my favorite coconut-almond milk or my special kind of black tea. The trash was always taken out and the lawn was always mowed. Everything was handled all the time. That's what I thought I wanted. Tom was the nicest guy on the planet. He would agree to anything, give me anything I wanted, do whatever I asked, eat whatever I chose. It was what I thought I wanted in a husband, so why had I wanted to claw his eyes out? What was wrong with me? Everything had been perfect with Tom, but I still felt miserable.

Seven years into our marriage, I still felt unlovable, and I was still constantly searching. My desperation turned to suicidal ideation, and I couldn't find relief for my pain—pain I didn't even know why I was feeling in the first place. I felt itchy and achy all the time—mentally, spiritually, and physically. Something was missing, and I just couldn't figure out what it was.

I had done everything right; I had done all the things. I was supposed to be happy now. I had a degree, a master's in business, and a great job in medical office management. I had a husband, a house, and a car. I even had a black lab with my favorite name, Lucy. I had checked all the boxes and climbed all the rungs of the success ladder, but I was still more miserable than ever. I couldn't stand it one more second. Seven years in— and two years after the weekend with Jason at Stagecoach Reservoir, I asked Tom for a divorce.

At 38 years old, I was starting over, feeling even more in a rush than I had at thirty. I was long past my marriage deadline, and I felt the pressure to be successful in every cell of my body. I wanted a husband I was attracted to, someone who would challenge me. I wanted more life and energy in my marriage, but all my efforts toward that goal had failed.

I felt like a failure every day around men. I felt like I had it together in all the other areas of my life, so why couldn't I figure this out? While getting ready for my weekend with Eric, I had packed more than just my belongings and Otis's supplies, as it turned out. Everywhere I went, I carried with me the baggage from my childhood trip to Sea World, the spankings, the camo Converse shoes, spin-the-bottle at Maggie's party, the frat party, and that night in the woods— and Jason's reaction at the cabin, too. All those experiences added up to decades of shoving down my pain, self-hatred, and suicidal ideation, and I was bringing them all with me on this trip.

I wanted to fix my deep wounds of unworthiness with Eric. If I could just get married and have kids, everyone would think I was good. Everyone would realize—*I* would realize—that I was lovable because someone loved me. I needed that more than anything.

Even in peaceful moments, like watching Otis bound around in a circle with the sun rising on a promising weekend, I could still feel the self-hatred and shame locked away inside, only temporarily at bay. As I watched Otis, my heart began to race. Eric pulled up in his black Toyota Tundra. It was happening. I had a feeling about this—a good feeling. It was all going to be okay. Eric was my answer to my prayers to belong, to be loved.

We loaded up his truck and lifted Otis into the back seat. He immediately put his little paws up on the window and looked out. His cute little face, so determined, exclaimed, "I'm a truck dog!" Even Otis thought this was the perfect fit.

I'd met Eric right after graduating from college. I'd known him for a good 20 years, and we chatted on the hour-and-a-half drive up to Steamboat Springs, flirting with each other the whole way. He was in the ski business, like my mom and brother, and we had so many mutual friends. He had always been there, weaving in and out of my life over the last two decades.

I had a sense that he had to be my person; he was the only guy that made sense. He was good-looking, tall with blue eyes that were nearly turquoise, blond hair, strong arms, and a ton of charm. *Why had I overlooked him for so long?* I wondered as we drove. *He was a nice guy—but was he too nice? Too normal?* I was so dysfunctional when it came to men, always preferring the ones who needed to be taken care of and didn't treat me well. But this was going to be different. Finally, it was going to work. He was nice, like Tom, but closer to my age, more attractive, and a better fit for me. It was happening! Finally, my life was coming together.

We pulled into the reservoir and got out the chairs and cooler. We shared a few cold beers as we sat by the lake and watched Otis work up the courage to swim. He'd run in, bark at the water touching his paws, and then run back out again. As the beer and Otis's antics relaxed my mind, I began to feel a release from my thoughts and all the scanning, worrying, and striving. I felt myself relax in the sun. This was good, so good.

We went for an afternoon standup paddle. I'd done it a few times, but Eric was a pro. I knew I was in good hands, and I looked forward to him giving me all the tips and tricks. He helped me get set up and I felt so special, so taken care of and seen. He was so sweet and attentive. I was relishing in it. We hopped on our boards and before I found my balance, Eric took off. *Wait,* I thought desperately. Before I was even stable on the board, he had zipped around the bend. I was alone in the lake, fighting to keep my balance and struggling to keep the feelings in the pit of my stomach at bay. This couldn't be a red flag, could it? This had to work. It was too close to perfect not to.

I swallowed my disappointment at the sting of being left

behind. For a few hours, I paddled by myself and played with Otis, staying close to the truck. I didn't feel comfortable leaving him or going too far out on my own. I felt so disappointed that Eric had just taken off without even checking to see if I was okay. That voice began warning me that something wasn't right, but I shook it off and didn't let my mind go there. I was having fun, damn it! Nothing was going to ruin my good time. I didn't want this to go wrong.

Eric came paddling back a few hours later with a proud smile on his face. He checked his watch and shouted out his paddle stats. He was so proud of his mileage and his time. But what about me? I didn't give two shits about his time or his stats. I was hurt that he bailed on me. But he was happy and didn't seem to notice anything, so I decided to let it go. *I'm sure I'm just overreacting*, I thought. *We're here to have fun—he obviously is, and I can, too.*

We dried off and noticed a couple nearby playing cornhole. "Oh, that's my favorite," Eric beamed as he grabbed another beer and headed over to introduce himself. Again, I felt disappointed. I thought this was finally our time to get to know each other and hang out. But I didn't want to be a bummer, so I grabbed a beer myself and headed over.

Before I knew it, we were playing doubles with this other couple. I was with the other guy and Eric with the girl. Not only were they were racking up points, but they were completely decimating us. My competitiveness and annoyance grew as they both sunk bag after bag. Every other time they'd scored, they high-fived and hugged each other. *Is Eric flirting with her?* I thought. Is he into her? *But she's married to this guy right here! What is happening?* Then, I noticed that while Eric was flirting with the girl, her boyfriend was all over me. *What the hell?*

I went along with it, not wanting Eric to think I was a prude or a bummer. As the drinks flowed, we were invited to check out their home, which was only a mile or so away. They asked us to play pool and hang out, and Eric's eyes lit up. He welcomed the invitation with what felt to me like an overly enthusiastic, "Yes!" Were the stars aligning? Were we meeting new friends with ease and grace? Or was something in my gut warning me that I was heading way off course?

At their house, I found myself outside on a lawn chair, playing with Otis with this guy putting his hands all over me. Soon, he was trying to kiss me. I felt all the stinging and shame of being raped come flooding in. My thoughts raced: *Am I doing it again? How have I been foolish enough to get myself in this situation? Where is Eric? Why did he ditch me again?*

I sprang up from the chair, feeling hot and tense all over, full of fear and anger. I hurried inside to find Eric. I followed the sound of laughter through the house until I found him leaning over the pool table, taking a shot with a huge grin on his face. As the pool balls clacked together, he stood and put his hand on the woman's shoulder. They laughed together happily. The heat and tenseness in my body intensified. Everything in me told me I needed to escape, now.

"Let's go," I said flatly.

"After this game," Eric replied, waving his hand and leaning on his stick, watching the woman set up for a shot. He looked so happy and chill. I questioned myself as I stood in the doorway shaking. *Why am I freaking out?* Eric hadn't really done anything wrong, and he was having a great time. *Why am I so weird? What is wrong with me?*

I went back outside, flopped down in the lawn chair, and started crying. Fortunately, the husband had gone inside to get more beer, so I didn't have to contend with him. Otis bounded over to me and whined, so I picked him up and held him close. He seemed to understand my pain. He snuggled up to my neck and I cried into his fur. After what seemed like a long time, Eric finally came outside.

"Okay, ready to go?" he asked cheerfully. When he looked saw that I was crying, his face instantly contorted with concern. "Are you okay? What's wrong?"

I couldn't hold it back anymore. I let all the frustration and disappointment of the day come rushing out. "Why did you leave me alone?" I cried. "I was scared and didn't know where you were." I sobbed between sentences, hiding my face in Otis's fur.

"What do you mean you were scared?" Eric asked, and I immediately felt stupid. I had no clear way to answer him. I didn't know in that moment why I had been scared, or at least I didn't know how to articulate it. I realize now, I was scared of being raped again. I was afraid of being left on my own. I was afraid of trusting Eric and making myself vulnerable again. I was terrified of our relationship not working out and of being left feeling worthless and hopeless. But I knew I couldn't say any of that out loud. Instead, I just wept.

We piled into the truck without another word, and all the way back to our hotel, I yelled at Eric. He fell silent and listened, trying to be supportive. When we got to our hotel, I brought in my things, got Otis settled, and completely ignored Eric. This was my go-to: shut down and ignore. I was already so good at ignoring my own thoughts that it wasn't hard to ignore someone else's. I trudged to the bathroom in silence, shut the door, and took a long, hot shower. When I was finished, I crept out and crawled into the queen-sized hotel bed. Eric was already lying down with his back to me, and I stayed as close to the edge as I could. I watched Otis sleeping in his soft crate on the floor next to me until I closed my eyes and drifted off.

I woke up the next morning to Otis crying in his crate. As I strained to open my eyes and reorient myself to where I was, the events from the night before started to return. I rolled over to find I was alone in the bed.

My thoughts began to race. *Did Eric leave me and Otis here? How would we get home? Was this ruined? Was this my fault?* All my inner dialogue of rejection, shame, and disappointment was mixing with the effects of a bad hangover. My head was splitting, my stomach churned with nausea, and I was beyond thirsty. I needed water. *Why did I drink so much?* I had been trying to cut down on alcohol, and I hated feeling so out of control. My list was full of unchecked boxes that morning, and I hated myself for every one of them.

I got up and gave Otis some food and water. As I walked to the other side of the bed, I nearly tripped over Eric, who was lying in a ball on the floor. He heard me startle and looked up at me, his eyes ablaze. The scowl on his face cut right through me.

"I didn't get any sleep at all," he shouted at me from the floor. "You were so out of line last night, Molly. The way you treated me wasn't fair, and now I'm beyond exhausted. I need to rest."

He hoisted himself off the floor, crawled into bed, and rolled away from me. My stomach felt like it was full of billiard balls. All I wanted to do was to go home, but I was stuck here, an hour and half away. I started considering people I could call to come get me but swiftly decided against it. I was too embarrassed to call anyone.

I took Otis for a walk and then hung out in the Holiday Inn Express lobby for a few hours. Otis and I found a plush, blue couch in a corner next to a coffee table and snuggled up together. He slept on my lap while I rotated through reading my book, playing games on my phone, searching Facebook, and drinking more complimentary cups of tea than was good for me. Staff and visitors trekked in and out of the lobby, always stopping to ogle and pet Otis, which made me less embarrassed to be camped out for so long.

It was about noon when I took Otis out again and went to find some lunch. We walked to a convenience store nearby, and I fought back tears as I wandered the aisles looking for food. Nothing looked appetizing. Eventually, I settled for a Lemonade Zero Vitamin Water and a chocolate chip Clif Bar. As the cashier scanned them through the machine, I realized the lunch represented how I felt—everything I did was just to get by.

I cried throughout the entire walk back as Otis ambled along beside me so innocently, and seeing him made my heart sink even more. I'd put him in this position. I'd put *us* in this position. I had ruined the trip, and now, we were stuck here. I considered walking home, but I couldn't do that to Otis. I would punish myself with a walk like that in a nanosecond, because I deserved it—but Otis didn't.

Around two o'clock, I returned to the hotel room. I turned the door handle as quietly as possible and stepped inside, Otis's claws tapping on the linoleum floor. Eric was still asleep.

"Eric," I said, my voice catching in my throat. I'd been waiting for him all day. I'd gotten up around seven in the morning, and I couldn't handle sitting in the lobby any longer.

"What?" he grumbled, still turned away.

"I need to go. I need to get Otis home. We can't hang out in the lobby any longer," I pleaded.

"Well, I didn't get any sleep last night. At all. I had to sleep on the floor, and it was freezing," Eric yelled.

"You didn't deserve that, and I'm really sorry," I replied. I felt so small, so alone, and so ashamed of myself. I wanted to disappear, and I began to cry again. "Can we please go?"

"Fine. I am really hungry," he said as he sit up, crossed the room, and rummaged in his duffel bag, all without meeting my eyes. "Let me shower and get ready then we can go get something to eat."

I felt some hope creep back in. Maybe it wasn't over. Maybe

Eric would give me another chance. Over the hours of loitering in the lobby and walking Otis, my anger had transmuted into shame. Then, just as quickly, hope had mutated into shame and desperation.

We found a great burger place in town and enjoyed some much-needed greasy food to soak up the alcohol from the night before. We didn't say much as we ate. I didn't know what Eric was thinking and worried that I'd failed this relationship as well. I was expecting to go home with my tail between my legs, another dream squashed. I scanned Eric's face and body language for clues about how he was feeling. Regret and agony churned inside me. I wanted a clean slate, to start over again, to pick up the dream where I'd left it yesterday.

We finished our burgers and hopped back into the truck. I held Otis on my lap to keep him safe—to keep *me* safe. He gave me security, like a safety blanket, a lifeline. As we drove toward the hotel, the suspense and tension built beyond what I could bear.

"So, what's the plan?" I said abruptly, cutting the silence.

"Well," Eric said with a pause I thought would last forever, "did you want to go home?"

Why was *he* asking *me*? Shouldn't he be making the decision about what happened next? He was the victim here. I was just waiting for the other shoe to drop.

"That's what I thought you'd want, after last night," I said, fear catching in my throat. I had braced myself for the inevitable breakup.

"I think we can pull up the choke on this weekend," he said, his voice flat and his face expressionless.

"What do you mean?" I asked tentatively when he didn't continue or clarify.

"We got a rocky start, but we have a fun weekend ahead of us, and I think we can recover. Let's stick with it and make it fun. What do you say?"

Relief flooded through me and I felt elated—I wasn't being rejected! I hadn't ruined it after all.

"Yes! That sounds great!" I exclaimed. I gave Otis an extra squeeze and reveled in the dream I had created for us in my mind. Maybe we *could* pull the choke up on this thing. Maybe we could try again.

I wish I had known what that expression really meant. At the time, I imagined lifting the flaps on an airplane, the ability to understand the situation with a little more altitude, a different perspective. I thought he meant, "Let's look at the bigger picture and see that this is just a small bump in a beautiful journey."

But pulling the choke restricts airflow—and from that moment on, driven by an overwhelming desire to keep things running smoothly, I decreased the air and pulled back on the oxygen.

Chapter 7

My Place

The next three years were more of the same—"pulling up the choke", prioritizing Eric's wants and needs over my own, and agonizing after every subsequent fight about it, with Otis there as a steady presence to comfort and ground me. A new career pursuit in pastoring became my aim, and I attended seminary, graduated, and started my work.

Ignoring my own intuition for the sake of making a relationship with Eric work, the two of us decided to get married. Only weeks later, I was appointed Senior Pastor at the United Methodist Church of Eagle Valley, checking more boxes in quick succession.

At the church, we had Wednesday night dinners, a weekly meetup for the congregation's women. I started to learn from others in ministry that it was part of the role of the pastor to host people at the parsonage. I'd heard of pastors organizing pizza parties, game nights, and Bible studies at the their homes, so it made sense when a group of friends from the church needed someone to host the weekly dinner.

It made sense for me to volunteer to host—not just because I was the pastor, but because I was the only one in the group without kids who needed to get to bed early. Thus, the tradition of a small group of women gathering at my house each week for salads, pizzas, and great conversation was born.

When we started, we went out to dinner a few times, but that became expensive, and going to someone's home felt more conducive to the level of conversation we were all craving.

I simultaneously looked forward to these dinners and slightly dreaded them. I'd heard the cautionary tales in seminary and from other pastors about keeping healthy boundaries with the congregation. I remembered that early in seminary, one pastor had told me to keep a strong distance.

"Don't let any of them into your personal life, ever," he warned. "You need to find friends in other places and keep work and your personal life separate."

In order to be a spiritual leader for the members of a congregation, a pastor needed to keep some separation and not become too enmeshed. In theory, this all made sense—but in practice, how could you work with people and live in community with them without becoming close? What did "friend" even mean? No one seemed to offer me clear answers.

How in the world could I separate myself that way? I put my whole heart into everything I did. I was the kind of person who became attached to a puppy in a commercial that was 20 seconds long—how could I spend years with so many amazing souls and not let them into my heart? I had wrestled with it since the beginning of my career as a pastor, and it still seemed impossible. What were the boundaries between a pastor and church member? It was another line to walk, and one of the most ambiguous I had yet encountered.

My mentor, the pastor at UMC Eagle Valley before me, was friendly with the entire congregation. He seemed to take the opposite approach from everything I'd heard, and he was beloved—every person I knew in the church considered him a friend. Again, I wondered where the line was. What was the right thing to do?

I feared I'd somehow crossed the line already, as I was very close with many people in the church even before I started serving as the pastor. What about my dear friend Deedy, who started attending when I began preaching? What about the advisory board, who felt like family to me? I was afraid of not being able to show up the way I needed to for others who needed me if I was too close to them, but was I already in too deep?

I thought about how physicians were not permitted to treat family, how they could actually do harm by being too close to the patient and not being objective. This was my greatest fear— that I might do harm. I didn't ever want to find myself in that position, and yet it was all so blurry.

I felt myself getting closer and closer to my faith community as the weeks passed, and I feared letting them down. I did my best to trust my heart, my intuition, and my faith. I had spent so much of my life feeling conflicted about myself that it was hard to distinguish intuition from fear. My intuition told me love was never wrong and to lead with my heart, but my fear reminded me that I should be constantly primed so as not to let my congregation down. I worried daily that the boundary was collapsing.

Despite my inner conflict, I liked having people over for Wednesday night dinners each week where I would order pizza and throw together a quick salad for everyone. I enjoyed the other women's company and hearing about the ups and downs of their daily lives, but any time I worried I might be getting too close, I would pull back. I'd spend the evening listening and not sharing much about my own life. Though I still enjoyed it, the distance began to make me feel inauthentic, and after a while, it felt like work.

Prior to seminary, I'd spent several years working in a community mental health clinic as a peer specialist. I sat with clients and listened, sharing my perspective and offering suggestions; this led to spending more than 10 years in community mental health working in suicide prevention and intervention. Through it all, I became skilled at listening to pain, holding space, and offering hope, love, and a listening ear. While I considered it to be my calling and my gift, when it was one-sided, it became energetically draining.

As a result of all the pressure, Wednesday night dinners eventually began to feel difficult. Holding space for others so late in the evening—after I'd already been doing it for most of the day and without an outlet for my own experiences—was hard. I considered these women friends, but it was a hard line to navigate. I found myself constantly juggling this conflict and testing the line, dancing in and out of connection with them.

Kelly Liken, a member of my congregation, added a new complication to my conundrum. Kelly was a celebrity chef and a big deal in Eagle County. She owned several restaurants and had done quite well on *Top Chef* and some other reality shows. She was also friends with my childhood friend Geoff Moser and his wife. I always like I was on the felt on the fringes of both friend circles whenever they collided. The Mosers and some of their friends were quite close with Kelly, and they often mentioned the "famous chef" they were friends with.

When I did meet her, I felt Kelly was somehow out of my league. Growing up as the nerdy, loser kid, I never felt like I was part of the popular crowd. Over time, I may have become friendly with someone who was more popular in school, but it was always clear to me that *I* was not popular. I knew my place. My role as the loser hadn't remained limited in the school cafeteria—it followed me into my own dining room in the parsonage of my church. I wasn't popular enough to be friends with someone like Kelly Liken. I knew my place, and I never tried to work my way in. Kelly would host parties for the Fourth of July, and our mutual friends would encourage me to come. I adamantly declined. I hadn't received a personal invite, and attending would make me feel like a huge imposter.

These boundaries started collapsing when Kelly started coming to my church. It was like the cool kid had suddenly decided to sit at my table. I quickly dismissed the idea that her decision had anything to do with me. Kelly wasn't coming to see me; she was coming to be a part of the congregation. These things were separate. When Kelly joined the Wednesday night dinners, I maintained my opinion: These women weren't coming to spend time with me as a friend, they were coming to see me as their pastor. They wanted connection to the faith community, to the Spirit, to God, and it had little to do with me.

It all kept me feeling emotionally distant from the group, and fro Kelly especially—but deep down, I delighted that Kelly Liken was not only coming to my church but to my house. I felt thrilled that we were spending time together. Her celebrity aside, I really enjoyed her company.

Wednesday night dinners started promptly at 5:30 p.m. and ended at eight o'clock; all the other women had kids in elementary school, so staying out late wasn't an option. Despite this, eight o'clock was a late night for me. Most days, I woke up between four and five o'clock, worked steadily all day, and was ready to wind down around seven and be in bed by eight. Wednesday nights were the exception, and I looked forward to them—not so much because of the dinners themselves, but because of the half hour between 5:30 and 6:00 p.m. Kelly showed up every Wednesday, right on time, while the others usually ran late and wouldn't begin to trickle in until at least six o'clock. So, for 30 minutes, it was just the two of us.

During those windows, Kelly and I would work together to get dinner ready for the group. As we threw together salads and ordered pizza, there was never any awkward space between us.

Conversation would begin as soon as she walked in the door and continue with ease for the rest of the evening.

During one of our chats, I pushed the boundaries a little and confessed to Kelly that by 5:30 on those evenings, I was beyond ready to eat, and it irked me that the others were always running late. Kelly had an easy solution: "We said dinner was at 5:30, so that's when we'll start eating." I thought I'd died and gone to heaven. Finally, someone understood me! I loved this about her.

From then on, we would start eating as soon as we were ready, often before the others arrived, and those weekly half hours with Kelly were one of the few spaces in my life where I could be myself, love what I loved, and need what I needed. Not only did Kelly make space for me to be myself, she actually *liked* my quirks. They began to crack something open in me beyond that my mind had never even imagined. Just by preparing and eating dinner with me, Kelly was teaching me how to be myself, which had always been my greatest longing in life.

Chapter 8

Dude Wipes

Most days, life felt like trying to put together an off-brand LEGO set. Every time I tried to add another brick—another grade, another accomplishment, another relationship—some previously constructed section would crumble. With each new brick, I lost a handful of others. Sometimes, I felt like I was almost there, with the finished masterpiece in sight and a happy life just up ahead.

I was recently married, I had been appointed to the church of my dreams, I had a group of good friends, and I was making a huge impact in the community. I prided myself on having everything together as if it were a vital part of my identity, and I hid my messes well. I always looked like I had my shit together, but I didn't. Oh, Lord, was my shit not together—not even close.

As a kid, not having everything organized and in its place was unacceptable. My brothers and I had checklists on our ski bags so we wouldn't forget anything, and my mom even made us travel notebooks. She helped us practice finding the gates, terminals, and know our way around an airport. We were trained to have our stuff together and keep it all buttoned up.

As an adult, that preparation meant that airport security had become the ultimate test for me: If I could get through without inconveniencing anyone, without being stopped or slowing down, then I passed. It was like a periodic screening of my shit-togetherness, assuring me that all was well—shoes off before the line, everything out of my pockets, no belt, no liquids, laptop out, bins in line. I had to have everything under control, and not just when I traveled. It was how I lived my entire life— but things were beginning to slip from my controlling grasp.

Eric and I had never been on solid ground with each other, but it seemed like we *should* be. Choking up that afternoon in Steamboat got us through the weekend, but we never fully recovered. I kept overriding my inner knowing, my boundaries, and all the signs and signals that we were not a great fit. I just felt like I'd come too far, I'd come too close. He must be the one I'd been looking for. He seemed to fit. He *had* to fit.

I had already filed for divorce from Eric once, only three months into our marriage, but I hadn't followed through with it. Still, it now felt like our marriage was really unraveling, and every cell in my body longed for a deep, true love.

Before I started dating Eric, it was as if that true love signal had suddenly been turned on high, and I couldn't stand it anymore: I had to find my person. I had been driven by accomplishing tasks and meeting goals my whole life, but finding true love felt different. I couldn't do anything else until that box was checked, and it felt like an addiction. Finding my person would be like getting the fix that would stop the screaming in my soul. I had to. Eric had to be the one; I couldn't wait any longer.

As this sense of urgency kept ramping up and I became more and more desperate, I loosened my boundaries and said yes to people, places, and things I never tolerated before. I dated guys online with whom I had nothing in common, even men who were more interested in drinking than anything else. I said yes to loud bars, late nights, and conversations that left me feeling misunderstood and unheard and like time was running out.

When our paths crossed again, Eric seemed like the answer to that urgency, so despite our difficulties, I had stayed and kept staying. From the start, our relationship had felt like a practice in not quitting, but it was getting harder and harder. I felt like a rope being pulled at both ends. Part of me was screaming to recommit, to lock in my person and finally belong. I didn't want to worry about being good or worthy enough to be married and to have a family, and I was desperate to put all the despair behind me. The pain of feeling like a failure was overwhelming, and Eric had to be the solution.

Still, another part of me was desperate to leave, to stop the fighting, heartache, suffering, and the feeling of being so alone. No one could see my pain, and I never wanted them to. Anything less than perfect was unacceptable, and it felt like I didn't have a choice. I was the senior pastor of a church; I couldn't get divorced *again*. What kind of leader would I be? I'd be letting everyone down. I'd rather let myself down and suffer.

One afternoon, feeling particularly on edge with these conflicting voices in my mind, I entered our Breckenridge home after spending a week in the parsonage in Eagle. I had often been returning to our shared home in Breckenridge for short stints, and the arrangement had seemed ideal at first. I considered myself extremely introverted and believed I needed time alone to recharge. As a pastor, I was with people most of the time, and I wanted to think it was the job that was draining me rather than my relationship with Eric.

The moment I walked through the door that afternoon, I scanned the house for anything out of place, anything to make Eric wrong. I didn't want to be there. I didn't like our house, and I hated that truth. I was a newlywed pastor, and I wasn't supposed to feel this way. I was supposed to be happy and blissful, loving being married and eager to come home to my husband. I wasn't supposed to feel this underlying pain anymore.

I was married, and married women were supposed to feel loved and beautiful. They were supposed to have a sense of belonging, so why wasn't it working? I wasn't happy, not even close, and I despised this about myself. I blamed it on Eric, because the more I could make it his fault, the more I could hide the fact that I had created the whole mess myself.

I had married someone I wasn't in love with. That was the truth I couldn't face. I hated how loud the voice in my heart and soul had become and that desperation had allowed to get me there in the first place. Now, the desperation was gone, replaced with regret, shame, and misery. No one could know. I could hold it together. I could make this thing work. I had to.

I marched through the living room—not even acknowledging Eric with a smile or a hello—into our bedroom and then the bathroom, spotting the overflowing trashcan as my irritation climbed. *Lazy*, I thought to myself, but that simple accusation was replaced with rage when I saw it: there, on the counter, was a package of Dude Wipes, and I felt my pulse throbbing in my temples as my jaw clenched.

My brother Willy owned a rental house in Vermont, and a few months earlier, Willy had struggled with renters using flushable wipes that clogged the pipes. Only after several months, many plumbers, and thousands of dollars had the issue been identified. I'd shared all of this with Eric, so I knew he knew better—why on earth would he bring these things into our home? How long had he been using them? Was the damage already done? Was the house going to flood again? We'd already weathered one flood in our house, and I couldn't bear another.

Idiot, I chided in my mind as all the pain of years of longing and frustration surfaced. My fear of being in the wrong relationship, of saying yes when it was a clear no, and all the suffering and yearning roiled in the forefront of my mind—all coalescing in this singular moment, the Dude Wipe debacle. It was as if Eric had punched me in the face.

I looked for more evidence, and it didn't take long to find it. I opened the cabinet under the sink and found a stash of over 40 packs of Dude Wipes. *Oh. My. Fucking. God*, I screamed in my head. It wasn't just one pack; he'd brought a Costco-sized pallet of these things into our house! I could imagine the pipes clogging and ready to flood our home at any minute. Suddenly, the pressure of my own clogged rage was about to make me burst.

I walked out of the bathroom in silent fury with the Dude Wipes in hand. I made my into the living room, ready to battle, where Eric was sitting on the couch. I seethed, the mere sight of him making me even angrier, even as his smile and eyes touched my heart and pissed me off even more. I wanted to be mad, to be furious—but his loving looks made me waver, which in turn had me at a boiling point.

Deep down, I wanted all of this anger, shame, and disappointment to go away. I didn't want to be this person. I didn't want this rage and hatred inside of me. I wanted to want him. I wanted to miss him, to race home and hug him, to enjoy his company. I wanted softness, nurturing, loving, and passion—shit, I'd settle for kindness. I could see a glimpse of all of this in him, in us. I knew he was capable of it, but it just wasn't accessible—so close, and yet so far away.

My heart strained at the contradiction, but my anger won out. I held up the Dude Wipes as if I was holding a dead rat.

"What are these?" I asked—I tried to keep a neutral tone, but there was nothing was neutral about it. Eric's face instantly turned red, and he started sputtering. He was struggling to find words, and this infuriated me even more.

"I use those for working out," he replied, stumbling over his words. "Sometimes I get sweaty when I work out, and I use those before getting back in the car."

He kept yammering about having used the wipes to clean up after paddling in the lake, insisting that he used them only for that and that he threw them in the garbage, but I knew he was lying to me. Every bullshit buzzer was going off in my brain. I had seen the overflowing trashcan, and there hadn't been a Dude Wipe in sight.

As I called him on it, he started trying to backpedal like a wounded animal. My heart responded as I felt sorry for him, and my instinct was to reverse course, comfort him, and avoid any further conflict. It was what I always did; I'd been a peacemaker my entire life, and it was my job to smooth things over, to keep the peace. I wanted to, but I couldn't. Not this time.

I wasn't ready to see that it was me who had said yes when it was a clear no. When *we* were a clear no. It was me who had forced this piece to fit. I created this, but I couldn't own that pain. It had to be Eric's fault, and the Dude Wipes were just the evidence I needed. I wanted to hurt him. That's hard to say, and horrible to own, but it's the truth. I wanted him to hurt just as much as I did. I wanted to take my pain of another failed relationship, another swing and a miss, of knowing I had not found my person, and put it on him. I wanted him to pay the cost of not being able to feed this longing. I wanted it to be someone's fault. Anybody's fault but mine.

Eric's lies got more outrageous the longer he talked, and I felt myself pass my threshold of self-control. Soon, it was my behavior that was outrageous, because I was raging, and it terrified me.

"I hate you!" I screamed, throwing my wedding ring at him.

All my suffering, longing, disappointment, and loneliness were surfacing as rage, and I was saying things to Eric I never thought possible. I didn't recognize myself, and I loathed that I was in this place. I hated what I was saying and how I was acting, and I couldn't believe I'd gotten here. I was a pastor, and yet I was screaming hatred at my husband. I was a fraud. I was unraveling. Who had I become?

"The only thing you're good at is leaving," Eric snapped as I stormed out of the room and slammed the door behind me. Everything that had ever been annoying or challenging in my life was churning together into an uncleanable, internal mess— and all because of Dude Wipes. It felt like a sunburn, and I couldn't stand to be in my skin.

I wanted to scream at the top of my lungs. I wanted to scratch all my skin off. I wanted to burn it all down and disappear. I couldn't stand myself, my marriage, my house, my life. I hated my husband, and I hated that I hated him; I didn't want to be capable of hatred, which just pissed me off even more. I felt like I was bleeding out, like my wounds were oozing uncontrollably and there was no bandage sufficient to save me, like everything was out of control. I didn't have one fucking thing handled, and I was terrified of anyone knowing.

Just like that day on the Comfort Inn bathroom floor, everything was leaking out of me on a minute-to-minute basis, even as I tried desperately to clean it or to hide it. It was staining everything, and I was running out of options, energy, or the ability to hold it all in. My life was falling apart, and it felt like there was nothing I could do to stop it.

Chapter 9

The Uncharted Exit

The winding drive back to Eagle mirrored the labyrinth of my emotions. Echoes of my intense confrontation with Eric were reverberating within me, the lingering effects of all the adrenaline manifesting in my hands trembling as they gripped the steering wheel. In a state of shock, I had found myself on the road, homeward-bound after a mere 30 minutes in Breckenridge, my plans of a weekend stay shattered. Once again, I'd departed prematurely, unable to cling to my intended itinerary.

Even before our fight, the duration of my visits to Breckenridge from Eagle had been dwindling each trip. I'd started to feel an odd sense of liberation in driving away from Eric, a conflicting admission that, despite its difficulty, carried an undeniable truth: a part of me yearned for my departures to inflict the same pain on him that I had continually endured. Leaving was becoming a silent act of retribution, a desire to mete out punishment. It made me feel a bitter satisfaction, mingled with the relief of freedom I felt every time I left to go home to Eagle.

But this time, any semblance of contentment was swiftly crushed beneath the stark reality of our crumbling marriage. The facade was cracking, and I knew I'd no longer be able to conceal what was really going on.

As the sting in my throat intensified and my tears demanded release, I glanced over to find Otis, my loyal companion, gazing at me from the passenger seat, his eyes conveying both understanding and unwavering love. His presence was a soothing balm, tempering the storm brewing within me. Behind the wheel, the gravity of my circumstances intensified, and any lingering doubt or uncertainty abruptly dissipated. Clarity emerged, stark and undeniable: *I am getting divorced.* The words reverberated in my mind, laden with the weight of what seemed like the ultimate failure.

Divorce. The very word resonated with both a sense of freedom and an undercurrent of panic, and I found myself caught in an undertow of emotions. The impending catastrophe I'd always imagined was transforming into an undeniable reality. Part of me fought to acknowledge that this perceived failure was, in fact, a significant step in my journey toward living a life true to myself. But another part of me, the louder part, was flooded with doubt and uncertainty. Divorce was a profound detour, a deviation from the path I thought was leading me to my best life.

For years, I had tried to convince myself that all the pieces were finally coming together, that the puzzle of my life was nearing completion. Now, it was as if someone had taken that near-finished puzzle and thrown it to the ground, breaking it into countless pieces.

"Why is this so hard?" I wondered aloud, my voice barely audible over the deafening noise of my inner turmoil and with tears streamed down my face. In the midst of this emotional storm, I glanced back over at Otis, thanking God for him. He was my one reminder in that moment that I wasn't alone, and his squishy face filled me with hope. *I can do this*, I thought. *I can walk this road.* I looked in the rearview mirror at the road stretching into the distance behind me with a profound realization. This journey to happiness I'd been on had been long and arduous, but, with Otis by my side, I was finding a reservoir of strength I didn't know I possessed. The journey through divorce, as tumultuous as it might be, would be my path toward authenticity and self-discovery.

I was halfway to Eagle when I rounded a particularly sharp curve and saw the road stretching ahead, and in that moment, I knew my marriage was complete. This clarity bathed me like the warmth of a sunny morning: I was done. My heart, now clear, acknowledged that I'd poured every ounce of myself into the relationship and there was nothing more to give. Of course, the weight of this realization was accompanied by a familiar companion: shame.

The cascade of self-doubt began. *I'm a failure. Divorced again. How did I get here?* My internal dialogue was relentless. *I can't make anything work. I'm not marriage material. Something is wrong with me.* It was suffocating. Eric's words at my parting echoed against the walls of my skull: "The only thing you're good at is leaving." A haunting thought began to take root that maybe he was right. *Maybe relationships aren't my forte and I'm better off alone,* I thought. *Maybe I'm not lovable in this way and it's been true all along.*

"At least I have Otis," I said into the silence.

A flickering reel began playing in my mind, flashing images of me having to claw my way through the daunting tasks that lay ahead. I'd have to tell Eric it was over—*that* dreaded conversation. Would I need a lawyer? The congregation was another layer of complexity. How could I let them down? How would I even begin to break the news? The hole in my stomach widened as the messiness of my life engulfed me. Had I ruined everything—again?

Memories of the messy aftermaths of so many failures consumed me as I drove. All my life I had questioned whether I would ever find a relationship, and any time I did, it had ended because of me, because of my inabilities. My forever fear of not finding love wasn't about companionship; it was a quest for acceptance and belonging. The fear of not being wanted had haunted me as a kid, through school, and into adulthood, evolving with changing rules but a consistent theme: the desperate search for a partner who would end the ache of not feeling valued, lovable, and wanted.

Marriage had become the solution, a desperate desire for a ring on my finger as proof of belonging. My first marriage, with Tom, had provided stability but couldn't fill the void, and the ache had persisted. This second marriage had held promise, but I had ignored too many red flags. As constant fights, avoidance of friends and family, and deep-rooted issues surfaced, I pressed on. The desperation to check the relationship box had overpowered my reason... again.

My desire to belong to someone who would love and accept me had always overshadowed the discomfort of compromising my authenticity, and my haste to bring that discomfort to an end always led to the same result. The pattern repeated: initial excitement followed by a realization of deep incompatibility. The pain of failure, shame, and confusion intensified every time. Why was I always unhappy? Was I destined to be alone?

As I pulled into the garage in Eagle, I felt a sense of peace, hope, and lightness rather than the disappointment and sadness I'd expected. Otis hopped out of the 4Runner and bounded into the house. He was on a mission to check his bowl, find his favorite red ball, and snuggle on the couch. I watched him and felt recognition. My soul wanted to bound into the house and rejoice in *my* life, *my* desires, *my* belongings. I'd forsaken myself to meet Eric's needs for so long. Suddenly, it was like I could breathe again.

I dropped off my bag in the walkway and headed to the kitchen. When I reached the doorway, I stopped and took it all in. The house was immaculate, just as I'd left it. The afternoon sun was streaming through the windows, bathing me in warmth, hope, and possibility. I opened the glass door to the deck and reclined on the patio furniture in the warm sun. Otis hopped up next to me and immediately fell asleep, so peaceful and content.

I sat there feeling his chest rise and fall. The life I thought I wanted was crumbling, and yet, I felt I was home, back on track.

A few hours after arriving home, I could no longer ignore Eric's persistent calls. I glanced down at my cell phone: 28 missed calls. *Seriously?* Taking a deep breath, I braced myself and finally answered the phone. Immediately, the harsh cadence of his shouting ripped through the line, triggering an instinctive response. Without a second thought, I hung up, unable to endure the onslaught of yelling. He called again and again, and I sat immobile, the constant ringing a reminder of the situation I was in. Ten minutes elapsed before I mustered the courage to pick it up again. This time, there was an eerie silence on the other end.

"I won't stay on the line if you yell at me," I asserted, drawing a firm boundary in the hopes of maintaining a semblance of control.

"Okay, I get it," he responded, his tone surprisingly calm, creating a momentary tranquility in the midst of the storm.

"We need to talk," I declared, preparing for the impending divorce conversation that I'd already been fighting on my internal battleground. "I can't do this anymore." The unexpected calmness in my voice surprised me. "I want a divorce."

These words had escaped my lips on numerous occasions during heated moments with Eric in the past, sometimes as a threat and other times as a fleeting glimpse of the truth. This time felt distinct. I sensed an irrevocable finality. This was the last time. I was done.

"No," he responded simply. "Molly, this is us. We can do this. We just need..."

I tuned out, having heard these assurances before—sweet talk, gentleness, promises that never materialized. He would say what I longed to hear, and I would relent. Not this time. Regardless of his words, I was resolute. We went back and forth. He wouldn't accept it. He persisted in arguing, pleading, and yelling. I listened for a while, holding my ground, until even that became untenable.

Interrupting him, I asserted, "Eric, I'm done. I want a divorce, and I'm hanging up now. I won't answer the phone again."

I ended the call. The phone rang persistently for several minutes. I refused to pick up. After a while, the ringing ceased, leaving behind an eerie quiet that simultaneously brought relief and an unsettling sense of finality.

Alone in the parsonage, I confronted the reality I had sought—freedom and solitude. The silence in the room was overwhelming, and I inhaled deeply, grappling with my complex emotions. The house had never felt so desolate or so safe. As I took in the details around me—the light shining through the curtains, my weekend bag discarded on the floor, an open book on the side table—I collapsed onto the couch beside Otis, curling up with him and holding on tight.

Chapter 10

My Person

I'd watched all 420 episodes of *Grey's Anatomy* at least three times. *Why am I so addicted to it?* I wondered. *Maybe watching the shit show that is the lives of the characters makes me feel a little bit better about my own.* More likely, it was the relationships the two main characters share that kept me coming back. Whenever I watched the friendship of Cristina and Meredith play out on the show, I wondered—could you have a designated person, someone *that* special? I had yearned for that, to be special to someone, but it never quite materialized. Where was my person? Had I ever had one? Did I have yet to meet them?

In the aftermath of that phone call with Eric, I knew he wasn't the one. Even so, sometimes, during our subsequent calls, I could hear the man I desired to love in his voice.

In the weeks that followed, Eric and I clumsily made our

way through every interaction. Sometimes, we even rekindled a familiar rhythm of kindness and friendship, as if trying to reclaim the camaraderie we once shared. It was comforting at times to have my friend back, but the fleeting nature of our affection always became apparent. The mention of divorce and selling the house reignited our dormant anger and bitterness, shattering any hope of an amicable split.

I struggled with that sense of transient harmony in so many relationships over the years. Leading up to my wedding with Eric, my best friend Taylor and I had broken apart. We'd met in Breckenridge working as medical assistants just after college and had known each other for 20 years. She'd known me better than anyone, and maybe that had been the problem—and the deal breaker had been light-up shoes.

I had been on the phone talking to Taylor about my wedding. I hadn't had a ceremony or reception for my first marriage, so I wanted a redo with Eric—I wanted to do all the things I hadn't been able to the first time around, and I was excited to talk to her and share my ideas. I wanted to get married at a ski area and have a big party. When I told her I wanted to have the wedding at the base of the mountain, she told me I should get married at the top.

I had a lot of really good reasons for wanting to get married at the base of the mountain. First, I couldn't get married at the top of the mountain because that's where I had married Tom. Getting married in the same place twice felt like a line I wasn't willing to cross. Besides that, the ski area wouldn't be open in the summer, which was when we were planning the wedding, so the lifts wouldn't be running, and getting everyone up to the mountaintop by car would be so difficult.

Logistically, it would be easier to accommodate the kind of party I wanted—food, music, and all—at the base. Even as I explained all this, I heard myself asking in my head, *Why am I arguing about this? I thought. Doesn't the bride just get her way? Why do I have to justify it?* I felt my irritation and frustration increase as she pushed back. Eventually we moved on to other details.

"What are you going to wear?" Taylor asked.

"Oh, that's easy," I replied, "something fun and a little bit out there, like light-up shoes."

"Absolutely not," she said. "That is where I draw the line."

What line? Why does she even have a say? After being questioned and feeling judged for my choices, I was beyond pissed. When I hung up, I was seething. Something stirred deep within me, and the pain felt familiar, old. Sitting in my car at the post office, I felt the heat of the day pounding on my face like an assault. *Why is the car so fucking hot? Why is there so much traffic? Why can't I make a left? And who gives a shit if I wear light-up shoes?* I ranted internally. *I'm so fucking sick of people telling me what I can and cannot wear. Isn't this the one time in my life I get to decide?*

When I was finally able to make the left out of the post office, my thoughts were at a full boil in the furnace of the car. The

Molly Booker

afternoon glare was intense, and I struggled to see anything with the sun shining directly in my face.

I remembered Taylor's hesitation and questions about my choice to accept the appointment to the United Methodist Church a few months earlier—where was her support? I was questioning a thousand things in my own mind, and I wanted someone to back me up—to help fuel my confidence, not my doubts. I was hanging on by a thread, and Taylor seemed to be pulling it loose rather than helping me weave things together.

In the midst of my second divorce, a season when I felt like I needed a friend more than ever, they just could not be found. Taylor and I weren't talking anymore, and my three other closest confidants at the time had all received a cancer diagnosis within months of each other. They were understandably unavailable, but I still felt so alone, misunderstood, and confused. I was lonely, and yet here I was pushing people away. I made no sense to myself.

So, I watched friendships play out on *Grey's Anatomy*. I wanted what Meredith and Cristina had. I wanted my person. How could I be so sure something was missing, so certain I needed that kind of connection, and why was it was so impossible to find? This fueled my conviction that there must be something wrong with me. There was no other explanation.

I found myself thinking about friendship a lot. I craved mutually fulfilling friendships but felt that so many of mine were out of balance. As a pastor, I gave so much to so many people, but I wasn't in a position to receive that friendship back. Like a therapist, these friendships had limits and boundaries. I

102

needed to be a pastor first, and that meant not always being a friend. It was a structure that pulled at my heart.

I continued to be plagued by not being able to fully connect with the Wednesday night dinner group. I often listened more than I spoke, and I offered suggestions and support without talking much about my own needs and struggles. This dynamic was great for my responsibilities as a pastor, but personally and as a friend, it was unfulfilling. I wanted someone who could access the full range of light and darkness with me, all of life's joy and despair.

I cherished my time with Kelly, but even those moments were limited—and there was still our complicated pastor-congregant relationship to contend with. I felt like I needed to meet her somewhere in the middle, leaving me feeling short of what my heart ached for and needed.

Strangely, even though I felt like I didn't have any friends, any time I went into town, people would stop and say hi. Most places I went, I knew someone. How did I know so many people and yet feel so alone? How could I feel such a strong sense of community and connection and yet still feel so isolated? How could I be so connected and disconnected at the same time?

Chapter 11

Depth

Out of breath, I came flying into the church fellowship hall a bit ragged and very sweaty. I had raced the elementary school kids into the church and, shocker, they all kicked my butt. As I came literally screaming into the building, thinking I'd find a room of kids all calling me a rotten egg, I instead found Kelly Liken, standing in the kitchen off the fellowship hall and organizing the kids' snacks. Equal parts embarrassed and shocked to see any adult, let alone her, I quickly changed my energy from eight-year-old to pastor. I straightened my hair and shirt, eking out a, "Hey there!" with a huge smile. I was surprised not only to see her but to realize how excited I was that she was there.

"Hi!" she choked out, not looking up from her task. I could tell immediately that something was off.

"Are you okay?" I asked.

"Yes—well," Kelly hesitated and mumbled. "Kind of, yes. Actually, no." Tears started streaming down her face. It was as if a waterfall of sadness came rushing off of her and covered me in it too, and I felt such compassion for her. I reached out and gave her a hug. She held on and we both just stood there. As I pulled back, she said, "We're moving."

"Wait, what?" I said dumbly. This made no sense at all. Kelly and her husband Rick were well-established in the valley and had just finished building their dream home. There was no way they were moving.

"Yep," she sniffed.

"Where?" I said, a bit louder than I had meant to.

"We're moving to Nashville for two years for Rick to do a residency," she continued. Her shoulders slumped in defeat. My brain struggled to catch up.

We both leaned against the kitchen island as if we couldn't stand up on our own. As we talked, I felt my back aching and struggled to find a more comfortable position. I put my elbow awkwardly on the island and adjusted a bit, glancing at the kids' drawings taped to the wall nearby. I couldn't help but pause at one particular drawing that Lucy, Kelly's daughter, had drawn herself—well, traced herself. The kids had taken butcher paper, traced themselves, and then colored the drawings in. Lucy's reflected her style perfectly–baggy shorts, big pockets, a hat, and pair of sneakers. I felt a sting in my eyes and my throat catch. I'd known Lucy since she was born, and now she was leaving? I'd always felt something special for her—a connection, something.

"A residency? Has this always been the plan?" I asked,

totally confused and seeing the frustration, and loneliness in her eyes.

"No, Rick just found out. I know, hard to believe, but yes, he just realized he needs to do a residency."

"Can't he do one in Colorado?" I asked.

"There are some in Denver, which is too far. I'm not willing to do the long distance again after doing that for his school. I want our family to be together, so we're considering it an adventure."

I wasn't sure if she was trying to convince me or herself.

I felt such a mix of emotions. First, devastation. It was strange; I didn't feel like we were that close, yet I felt such a loss that Kelly was moving to Tennessee. *Couldn't it have been anyone else? Why her?* There was also a bit of excitement for her about this opportunity, as I loved a story of transformation and change. My favorite novels were the ones about breakups, someone getting fired, a death—and the resultant transformation, rebirth, and reinvention. I even felt a bit envious of her.

But I also felt relief. Her move would open a window for friendship. If Kelly was no longer part of my congregation, we could cultivate a closer connection. I wouldn't need to worry as much about maintaining the pastor-congregant boundaries.

The summer passed too quickly. I was busy with the church kids' programs, working on the yearly worship, and the church schedule and calendar. I saw Kelly a few more times before she left. She seemed to be handling it all with such grace. She was packing up her home, buying a new one in Nashville, renting out hers, getting Lucy enrolled in school—how was she doing it all? It seemed overwhelming to me with all the moving pieces, but each time I saw her, she always seemed like she had it handled.

Rick and Kelly had a going away party, and I debated about going. I knew the family well, so going and saying goodbye made sense, but a part of me felt I wasn't invited or welcome. It was the old part of me that always felt that Kelly was out of my league, like I was not part of her circle. I quickly talked myself out of going, which felt both relieving and disappointing. Much like missing prom and other important school events when I was young, I was glad that I didn't have to endure the social anxiety and awkwardness, but I always ached at feeling I was missing out because I didn't belong.

After Kelly and Rick had moved, I heard from some mutual friends that Kelly was really having a hard time. Rick had quickly made friends at work, and Lucy found her place in the new school, but Kelly was mostly at home alone, unpacking and getting the house set up. I felt a pang of hope as the opportunity for a call opened up.

I texted Kelly saying hi, telling her I was thinking about her, and asking for a time we could talk. She immediately texted back, and we messaged back and forth for quite a while. We agreed on talking early in the morning via video chat, a technology that felt new and unfamiliar to me, formal and intimate at the same time. I was going to be able to see Kelly and talk to her in the morning. I wondered why I felt somewhat nervous, but I figured it must be because I was still a bit starstruck around her.

As soon as her face popped up on the screen, I scanned the room behind her. It was like I was on a scavenger hunt, desperate for clues about her new home and her new life. We talked about her loneliness, and I really felt her pain. I knew that emptiness, and I could only imagine how hard it was starting over in a new place, knowing no one. I felt bad and wanted to take the pain away, which led to a conversation about a visit to Nashville. I quickly agreed. I bought a plane ticket and put the trip on the calendar, the ultimate signifier that something was definitely happening. I was set to visit Kelly Liken during Thanksgiving break.

In October, I went to Florida to visit my mom and dad. I took pictures of the beach, the palm trees, and us having a great time in the hot sunshine and sent them to my brother Willy, in Vermont. I raved about how wonderful it felt to get warm and feel a piece of summer at the start of winter. I must have sold the idea, because suddenly Willy and his wife were booking tickets to Florida for Thanksgiving break. I felt if Willy was going to be with our parents for Thanksgiving, I wanted to be there too, so I canceled my trip to see Kelly. It's a rare thing to spend a holiday with my family, so it felt like an easy choice at the time, but I felt so bad letting her down. I so didn't want to disappoint her, yet disappointing my mom and dad would feel so much worse.

Without fully realizing it or understanding it, canceling on Kelly weighed on me in the following weeks. I thought I just felt bad about ditching her, but I knew it was something deeper. The feeling persisted, and I distanced myself from her. She reached out many times over the next several months, but I didn't engage. I had become an expert at creating distance, especially when I needed closeness, but I didn't see it at the time. I can hardly remember those months. It feels odd to have such a block when it comes to those weeks and weeks thinking about Kelly. It's like someone went into my brain and edited out the parts with her in it.

Several of the women from our Wednesday dinners filled me in that Kelly and her family were coming back to town. Again, I felt strangely numb about this information. Why did I feel so disconnected?

Kelly had been in and out of my thoughts for a week or so when I received a text from her saying:

Hey! Lucy and some of the other kids are going to camp in southern Colorado. I rented a Vrbo, come join!

I felt extremely torn. I wanted to see Kelly and connect the way we had during our Wednesday dinners, but I couldn't come and stay with the other women from church.

Clearly, that would be stepping over the pastor boundary. I struggled to find the words to text back. I attempted a few and quickly deleted them. Why was I having such a hard time saying no? Finally, I went with the truth:

Hey, thank you for the invite. It means more than you know. While I'd love to come see you, being in the position of all these women's pastor, I just can't. It puts me

in an awkward position and I think I need to say no.
Sorry to miss you!

Three dots immediately popped up after I hit send. She was typing something. *What is it?* I thought anxiously. *Is she upset?* I so wanted her to understand. She responded:

Oh bummer. I'd love to see you, but I get it. Lucy and I
are going to stay a bit longer. I'll be up in Eagle. Want to
grab breakfast?

This was perfect. I'd be able to see her after all, and this was much more my speed. I put it on the calendar and felt eager every day that passed. As fate would have it, on the morning of our breakfast, it seemed like a million things were vying for my time. Someone needed something at the church, someone else needed a ride to the hospital for an appointment. While I normally would quickly cancel my plans to take care of others, this time I didn't. I told each person that I was busy for the next few hours and would be happy to help after that. I held my boundaries. Saying no and risking others' disappointment was so hard, but something about it felt right.

Kelly and I met for breakfast at the town diner and shared an omelet. Kelly ordered, and I trusted that as a chef, she would know just what to get. I wasn't wrong. The veggie omelet was amazing, and she asked for the hash browns extra crispy, just as I liked them. It felt intimate to have breakfast with just Kelly, especially because we were sharing food.

It felt so comfortable, a stark contrast to how I usually felt in one-on-one situations. I felt so at ease with her. We talked about seminary school and all the courses I was taking on justice, race, and gender. I felt like I could ask her questions that I hadn't been comfortable asking before about race, gender expression, and sexuality. Her daughter, Lucy, both being mixed-race and expressing her gender in a more masculine way, felt like a bridge to Kelly, whose presence seemed like a safe place to air out my questions and uncertainty.

While we talked about Lucy, it strangely felt so personal. I wished as a kid I'd had the freedom that Lucy did to wear boys' clothes and cut her hair short. Why did I always feel like such a failure as I leaned toward more masculine gender expression, but for Lucy, it came out as confidence? Our conversation covered may topics, and I knew I wanted to spend more time with Kelly, Rick, and Lucy. I agreed to come visit them in Nashville, and Kelly teased me about cancelling on her. I promised that, this time, I would be there.

I rescheduled for August of the next year. Again, I booked the ticket and put it on the calendar. This time I didn't cancel.

I spent several days in Nashville with Kelly and her family. The thing that stood out most to me was the depth and frequency of our conversations. In previous friendships, I usually felt like I was the one not just initiating conversation but encouraging and pushing for depth, yet it was Kelly who led during our time together. I remember feeling surprised at how much we were talking and at our level of intimacy. We spent most of the trip walking together, exploring the city, and weaving our way through the most fascinating, enlightening conversations. Eventually, we found our way back to Lucy and her gender expression. I opened up, allowing myself to share my childhood pains of not being able to wear what I wanted and being teased as a tomboy and called gay. I hadn't talked about these things with anyone before—why was all of this surfacing now? Why did it keep coming up with Kelly? We talked about books, growth, values, what we wanted, and a lot about seminary and my next steps in ministry.

The depth of our conversations caught me off guard. I remember wondering while I was in Nashville whether Kelly could be a close friend. Obviously, there was some level of friendship there already—I had flown across the country to visit her. I almost felt like I was interviewing her during that visit, like I was testing the waters to see if she could go to the depths. Could she be the friend I was looking for? The friend I had so badly needed these last several months—and for a lifetime?

Among the deeper topics we explored was our love for music. I told Kelly I was on a "personal farewell tour"—I was trying to see as many musicians in concert as possible, particularly those I thought would be retiring soon. Elton John, James Taylor, and Journey were a few that made the list.

Kelly seemed stoked at my plan. "What a cool idea! Who else is on your list?"

I still wanted to see Madonna, Bruce Springsteen, and Cher, to name a few. On several occasions, Kelly brought this up and said she was going to start doing this as well. She was so enthusiastic about it, and I loved that she was so excited about

Molly Booker

something I found so much joy in. This was something we could share.

After I returned home, we texted back and forth a few times, but her responses felt lackluster. I could tell something was upsetting her. One day, I texted her before anxiously waiting for her response:

Are you okay?

She texted back:

Not really.

I felt my stomach tighten.

OMG, what's going on?

Finally, she replied:

We don't need to get into it, I'm okay.

I thought we had gotten close in Nashville. Why didn't she want to tell me? I felt so helpless, so far away, and I wanted to help take the pain away. How could I when I didn't even know what the pain was? Was it Rick? Where they fighting? What was going on? I felt so in the dark.

I reached out a few more times the next week. I could tell Kelly was really going through something, but she didn't seem

114

to want to talk about it. I appreciated our back-and-forth texts, but I felt distanced.

In the midst of my confusion, she sent me another text one day out of the blue:

I'm headed to Denver to see Robert Plant play with Alison Krauss at Red Rocks on Thursday. I'm going with Jenna and she has an extra ticket. Want to come?

Yes, of course, I thought. But also, *Wait, what? She's coming to Colorado? Are we still close, then?* I was filled with uncertainty and eagerness to see her again, competing inside me like a cacophonous drum solo.

I didn't know much about Robert Plant or Allison Krauss, but Kelly was excited about it, so I played along. Somehow, even though I had been born and raised in Colorado, I had never been to a concert at the iconic Red Rocks venue. Even if I didn't end up enjoying the music, at least I'd get to go to Red Rocks. At least I'd get to spend more time with Kelly. Finally, I replied:

Hell yes, I'd love to.

Chapter 12

The Pants-Whisperer

E ven as the day of the concert grew closer, the spark we had in Nashville seemed to fade. Kelly became more distant, and our conversations grew strained. I couldn't understand what had shifted. Was it me? Was it something I said or did?

I tried to reach out a few times, but the responses were brief and lacked the warmth we once shared. The weirdness between us grew, and I found myself questioning the authenticity of our connection. Was I just a temporary companion filling a void during a challenging time in her life? The confusion lingered, and I struggled to reconcile the vibrant friendship I had envisioned with the reality unfolding before me. Maybe I had misunderstood the signs, or perhaps the universe was playing a trick on my longing heart. Friendship, it seemed, remained elusive, leaving me with the same ache for connection that had haunted my past.

Despite the weirdness, I still met Kelly not long after at Avanti, a food hall in Denver near the Red Rocks venue. I was excited to see her again, but I was plagued with doubts about why she had asked me to go with her to the concert. It always seemed to me that Kelly had many friends and usually hung out with a big group. Why would she care about me?

Jenna, a longtime friend of Kelly's, had picked her up at the airport, and I was supposed to meet them for lunch before going to our Vrbo. I felt nervous walking into Avanti as I scanned the crowd to find them. The place was brimming with people, their noisy conversations and easy camaraderie overloading my brain. Surrounded by people and imagining Jenna and Kelly sitting at a table together enjoying each other's company, my fears about being the loser plagued me: *Am I showing up too early? Will they think I'm a dork? Did I park too far away? Will I know where to find them? Will I look stupid walking in by myself?* I felt like I was thirteen again, walking into the cafeteria alone. It felt like everyone in the room was staring at me, seeing my lack of belonging as easily as they'd spot a pair of camo Converse shoes.

I finally spotted Kelly and Jenna through the crowd. After hugs and smiles from Kelly and an awkward hello with Jenna, I sat down. My uncertainty continued. The two of them already had food. *Should I go get some? Are they waiting on me? What should I eat? Will they judge me?* I was so frustrated at my awkwardness. I felt like a teenager.

Eventually, I got up and ordered some tacos and a Diet Coke. I felt so self-conscious but tried to play it cool. I worried they would think I was dumb for ordering a Diet Coke. I tried not to drink too much of my soda and fretted the whole time, wondering if Kelly would judge me for my unhealthy choice. I agonized over my meal, even after it was consumed.

Jenna headed out to meet another friend before the concert, and Kelly and I left to go find the Vrbo. I mulled over how to ask her if we could go to REI first, which was close by, so I could get some hiking pants. *Surely, she won't mind—but will she? I thought. Should I ask her? Ugh, am I being weird?*

As we neared the car, finally I blurted the question. "Of course," Kelly replied, sounding delighted. Things were so hard with Kelly, but they were so easy, too.

As we walked around REI, it felt like a bonding experience. We chatted about outdoor gear, hiking, and our favorite places to explore. I felt my body relax as we walked and talked, the Diet Coke drama long forgotten.

My inner turmoil turned instead to the task of finding pants. Finding pants I liked was a struggle. They were always way too long, or too tight, or fit too high on the waist. I felt self-conscious about my pickiness as I searched the racks for something, anything that would fit the bill. With four pairs of pants draped over my arm, I went to find the dressing room, huffing in frustration with each failed attempt. Suddenly, Kelly's shoes appeared in the space between the floor and the changing room door.

"Why don't you try these?" she casually asked, slinging three more pairs over the doorframe.

Mechanically, I grabbed the hangers and pulled the pants into the changing room, unsure what to say. Any time I'd shopped with a friend in the past, they would go shop for themselves while I tried on a few things, and inevitably I'd leave empty-handed because nothing felt or looked right.

I felt confused—why was she being so nice to me? It was weird that I got skeptical when someone was nice to me, but when people acted like assholes, I felt no alarm. I almost expected people to disappoint me and was reminded of it as I questioned Kelly in that moment—but the wildest part was that the three pairs of pants she had brought to me were perfect.

"You must be the pants-whisperer!" I joked, trying to sound casual despite my genuine awe.

I bought all three pairs. They're still my favorites.

Chapter 13

Concert Confessions

After that miraculous moment at REI, we picked up Jenna and drove to our Vrbo. The directions were a bit confusing and it was hard to tell if we were in the right place. We parked in a dirt lot behind the Vrbo that was next to a dumpster. I worried whether I was too close and would get towed. *Why am I always so worried about everything?* I chided myself internally.

Kelly led the way up some steep wooden stairs, and we wondered together if we were in the right place. Kelly punched in a code on the lock, and just like that, the door was open. We walked down a tiny hall passing several apartments with funky art on the walls and decorated doors that reminded me of college dorms. Eventually, we found our door and walked in.

The place was amazing. It had a modern feel with funky metal stools, cozy couches, and tons of open space—but as the three of us stepped inside, I felt some of my social anxiety surface. Kelly, Jenna, and I would all be staying here after the concert. There was one room with a queen bed and another room with two bunk beds. I watched as Kelly threw her stuff on the top bunk without a second thought. I wanted to be in the same room as her. Maybe we would stay up late talking, like a sleepover. *Will she think I'm weird if I put my stuff on the bottom bunk? Does she want Jenna to sleep in here? Why am I so nervous!* Usually, I'd claim the single room with the bigger bed — I was such a light sleeper, and I always went to bed before everyone else. Typically, I wanted quiet and lights out by eight, yet here I was, daydreaming about a sleepover with Kelly.

As she rummaged through her bag, I tossed my things onto the bottom bunk. She didn't say anything. I wondered how she could seem so cool about things—lunch, shopping, rooming together—when I was such a wreck. On the way to the concert to tailgate, as we sat in standstill traffic, I felt myself getting annoyed. I worried we wouldn't be able to find a place to park. *We should have left so much earlier*, I thought. As always, my brain was running—worrying and looking for something to stress about.

Despite my usual agonizing over things, everything worked out without any hassle. As we set up our chairs and the food that we brought, everyone started to dig in—between Kelly and Jenna, who was also a chef, it was quite the spread. Usually, I would've only prepared some chips and dips, but what we had was more like a tapas restaurant! We had cheeses whose names I couldn't even begin to pronounce as well as meats, mustards, salads—the works. Each bite was more delicious than the last, but Jenna's homemade pickles were over the top. As I chatted with Kelly, Jenna, and Jenna's friend, I could not stop eating those delicious pickles, and Kelly and I battled it out for the last one.

Eventually, the carefree enjoyment gave way to ruminating. I noticed myself feeling frustrated with Kelly, but I couldn't figure out why. It almost felt like disappointment, but at what? What was I wanting or expecting? I had no idea. I felt myself distancing myself from her and chatting with Jenna instead. It was just like the game I'd played in the dating world—act aloof or uninterested to change the dynamic, and they'd come right to you. I found a sense of ease talking and laughing with Jenna, and I found myself looking to see if Kelly noticed. I was trying to make her jealous. It was totally unnecessary and yet felt weirdly imperative in the moment.

When we parted ways, Jenna and her friend took their seats up front near the stage, and Kelly and I went to ours near, the top of the amphitheater. I felt relieved and excited that it was just us sitting together, with the group dynamic and its strange effects on me behind us. I was getting Kelly all to myself, and that felt special. Settling into my spot beside her, I wondered, again, why she had invited me. Kelly had a lot of friends, and she was practically a celebrity. She could've had an entire group of people here without any problem. Aside from my time in Nashville, those thirty-minute chats we'd had during Wednesday night dinners were pretty much the only alone time we had ever had—Kelly was always surrounded by friends. I loved knowing she had invited me and me alone to the concert, but I felt self-conscious at the same time.

The music was great, and it could have been a wonderful experience—"could have" because my brain was still going into overdrive. There was a couple in front of us necking, and I couldn't stop looking at them. It took me back to my school days, looking on while couples made out in tunnels on the playground or in the student section of the bleachers, feeling simultaneously annoyed at their PDA and intensely jealous. Annoyance and jealousy spiraled into overthinking and ruminating. I began to worry about getting home. *How late are we going to stay? What if I get really tired? What if the concert gets boring?* I would have enjoyed the music if it weren't for the anxiety reel flickering in my mind.

I kept joking with Kelly about the couple necking. It felt like a safe common ground. I felt so nervous sitting with her at the concert. I worried I would run out of things to say or not be cool enough to justify her invitation to be there in the first place. It was nice to have the distraction of the music and not feel like I had to keep the conversation flowing the entire time. Occasionally, I'd lean over and talk right into her ear so she could hear me over the noise, and she'd smile and laugh in response. I wasn't totally blowing this; we were having fun.

She asked if I was ready to leave about halfway through. Thank God I hadn't had to figure out how to navigate asking to leave. We strayed lower into the amphitheater, found Jenna, and headed out. We stayed just long enough, had a great time, and kept up good conversation on the drive back to the Vrbo. I didn't quite get the sleepover I had dreamed of—I fell asleep as soon as I hit that bottom bunk.

I woke up the next morning just in time to see Kelly leaving our room with her running shoes on. My heart sank. I would've gone for a run with her if she'd asked—she should've known that about me. I felt the sting, but quickly recovered, buoyed by our experiences from the day before.

I took that happy energy with me as I left to go to a nearby coffee shop. The shop prepared my drink perfectly—English breakfast tea with a dash of coconut milk and a dash of almond milk. I had a great chat with my mom on the phone on the way back to our Vrbo, perfect tea in hand and a contented smile on my face. With all anxieties forgotten, the day was filled with possibility. I'd wait for Kelly to return from her run and see what the day would bring. I took another sip of my tea, then headed inside.

As I reached for the doorknob to the room with the bunkbeds, my heart sank. I heard Kelly and Jenna talking in the other room. Kelly was crying. She wasn't out running; she was going through something, and she was confiding in Jenna, not me. My stomach tightened, turning the tea in my stomach to acid as disappointment flooded my entire body. Along with the dejection of knowing she hadn't confided in me, I remembered the unspoken words from our text exchanges over the last couple weeks.

I knew there was something going on, probably with her husband. I assumed that's why she had wanted a getaway to Colorado. I couldn't understand why she hadn't felt like she could talk to me. We'd spent plenty of time in the car together on that bonding trip to REI, and we'd even shared a room together. There had been plenty of perfect opportunities to open up about whatever was going on. Sitting in the living room waiting for Kelly and Jenna to emerge, I felt awkward and left out, my cup of tea growing cold in my hand.

Fortunately, I worked my way quickly out of the rabbit hole. I was getting good at minimizing the "down" times. I had been practicing to feel the hard emotions—anger, jealousy, sadness, disgust—and move through them quickly. First, I checked in to identify my emotions. I was feeling disappointment and jealousy. I was jealous of Jenna and feeling the loss of not connecting with Kelly over whatever it was that had upset her. I also felt confusion. Maybe I was wrong about our new friendship. Maybe we weren't becoming as close as I thought. I was strangely okay with this idea and reached acceptance quickly.

I had come to Denver with the intention of building a new friendship with someone who could go deep and hit the range of highs and lows with me, and maybe it just wasn't Kelly. It was like trying on a pair of hiking pants that looked perfect on the rack, but then in the dressing room, they didn't quite work. You just put them back and tried another pair until you found the right one. That was the space I was in: a bit bummed, but okay. Kelly had known Jenna for 20 years or so. It made sense she would turn to her when things got rough.

I set my tea on the coffee table, feeling resolved as they both emerged from the bedroom. I could see that Kelly wasn't trying to hide that she'd been crying, but it had stopped by then.

Neither of them talked about the fact that they had been in the bedroom at all or that Kelly had been crying. They skipped over it, and I took their lead. We began creating a plan for the day.

The original plan was for me to take Kelly to the airport later that afternoon. I started to say I was still happy to do that, when Kelly said simply, "I don't think I need you to take me to the airport today."

"Are you sure?" I asked.

"I'm sure. I think I'm going to stay another day."

"Oh, that's awesome," I replied. I waited for more direction, glancing at my abandoned tea. I was confused about where I fit in here. Did Kelly and Jenna want me to excuse myself and drive home?

"I'm happy to do whatever works for you," I said. "If you want time to yourself, I'm happy to drive you somewhere, or if you want to talk, I'm up for that too. If you just want to hang out, I'd be down for that as well. You just let me know what you need." I was rambling, but I had to fill the empty space.

"Yeah, I'd just like to hang out," Kelly said quickly.

"My family has a cabin in Boulder Canyon on Boulder Creek. She might go there," Jenna offered. "Kelly, I can drive you. Or my aunt can take you! We'll just figure it out—"

"I'll take you!" I blurted before my brain had a chance to process any of this at all. I was surprised at my quick answer. That wasn't usually like me. But it was true. I did want to continue to hang out, and a cabin sounded really fun.

Jenna rubbed Kelly's back, then scurried back into her room. I heard rustling and the groan of zippers and moments later, she came bustling out of the room with several bags in hand, which were falling over and things were spilling out. This would have frustrated me beyond belief, but none of it even made Jenna pause. I knew Jenna was an urban farmer and that she was excited to get back to her chickens, plants, and farm projects. She radiated joy and didn't seem to care about the small things; I was even a bit envious of Jenna's free spirit.

Before she left, Jenna gave us the rundown about how to open up the cabin and couldn't stop gushing about how excited she was for us to use it. After that, Kelly and I went our separate ways for a couple hours. I ran some errands and met Kelly after breakfast, and we decided to go for a walk in a nearby park.

I thought walking would give Kelly a chance to share anything from earlier if she wanted to, but she kept directing the conversation toward me. I shared my concerns about seeking ordination in the church. I was nervous to commit and wasn't sure if it was really something I wanted to do. It also didn't land for me that there were so many of my gay colleagues not able to make it through this process. Should I use my privilege of being straight and cisgender to use the system to help change it? Or should I not participate in such an inequitable system? I didn't have easy answers. Neither did Kelly, but she was an apt listener and supporter.

We soon gave up on walking in the heat and went to lay under a tree. I studied the tree so intently that I can still picture its branches and leaves. Soon, the conversation meandered into having "a person."

When I mentioned my fascination with *Grey's Anatomy*,

Kelly exclaimed, "Me too!" I was almost too embarrassed to bring it up, but apparently, she was a *Grey's Anatomy* nerd too.

"I don't think my husband is my person," she confessed, then sniffled.

In the brief silence that followed, I felt almost excited, which alarmed me. Coincidentally, I had just learned the word *schadenfreude*—experiencing pleasure in response to another's misfortune—and here I was experiencing it. When I had first heard the word, I quickly declared this would never be something I would do. In the moment though, I realized my Denver Broncos tattoo was a permanent reminder of how much pleasure I feel any time my team sacked another quarterback. The more I thought about it, I was horrified to realize how often I delighted in other people's misfortune.

When I got a green light and went happily on my way, I was almost encouraged that someone else was stuck at a red light. If someone dropped some money and I found it on a sidewalk, I thought of it as a win for me because it was a big loss for someone else. All this bounced around in my head while lying on the grass next to Kelly. Here she was confiding that maybe her person isn't the one she married, and something in me delighted in it. Simultaneously I wondered, *Am I a monster?*

I confessed that my husbands—cringing at the plural—had not been my people. Eventually Kelly said quietly, "I think you might be my person."

I lost my breath. My heart began to race. I wasn't crazy—there was *something* here. Elation danced inside of me. *Fuck yes*, I thought. I felt like I'd just scored a touchdown in the Super Bowl. "I think you might be my person too," I responded, my stomach flipping.

Maybe Kelly was my person. Maybe I did have a Cristina after all. Was she what I had been missing—a best friend to do life with? Was this longing, the perpetual feeling that something was missing, almost over?

Chapter 14

No Longer Alone

I rode the wave of elation for the remainder of the afternoon. There was a newfound intimacy between Kelly and me. That moment under the tree sparked something inside me that had long been extinguished, perhaps never even existed before. Something was different.

As we headed up to Boulder, stopping by the grocery store for provisions, I felt a shift. I wasn't alone, not in the conventional sense, but rather, I had a partner—a teammate. It was a different feeling, one that contrasted sharply with the solitary path I had navigated for much of my life.

During family vacations, I often found myself alone—a solo traveler in a crowd. While others enjoyed the comfort of their own rooms, food preferences, and a sense of belonging, I remained on the periphery. My life had been marked by a perpetual sense of not quite fitting in or belonging. For the first time, that feeling eluded me, and the inexplicable change baffled me.

During our stop at the grocery store, Kelly made a conscious effort to pick up my favorite Almond Breeze coconut-almond milk. How did she even know it was my milk of choice? It felt as though she was planning a special meal just for me, looking out for me in a way that transcended the ordinary. Typically, in the company of friends or family, each person would grab a basket and retrieve what they individually needed. This time, it was a single basket, and Kelly was helping me gather what *I* needed—unfamiliar, but welcome. Was this what having a person felt like? It was indisputably different. A warmth, a thawing, a strange hopefulness enveloped me. I felt excited, joyful, and, above all, comforted by hope. I couldn't quite comprehend the shift, but it felt undeniably good.

The journey to Jenna's family cabin involved a long and winding road, leading us outside Boulder and into the canyon. The road grew narrower, transitioning to dirt, and my initial nervousness returned. *Had I chosen the wrong car? Could I navigate this terrain?* As we drove, I checked my phone to find I had no reception. Rather than redouble my anxiety, the loss of cell reception strangely pleased me; for about twenty-four hours, Kelly was mine alone. The idea of just the two of us excited me.

But as we drove deeper into the woods, my anxiety heightened. *What if the road worsens? What if we're trapped?* The cabin's isolated location made me uneasy, as I hadn't informed anyone of our impromptu trip. The secrecy felt unsettling—a bit risky but invigorating at the same time—and my conflicting emotions puzzled me. Logically, I thought to myself, *I'm with my friend, Kelly.* But I knew there was something else there, too.

The feelings clashed with my rational mind. When we reached the cabin, I exhaled with relief. The drive wasn't as challenging as I had feared. My anxiety, per usual, stemmed more from potential difficulties than the actual road before me. Fear, I realized, often revolved around future events appearing real—concerns about what might happen rather than the present circumstances.

The cabin, an enchanting A-frame with expansive windows and a cozy porch, brought back memories of my childhood home in Evergreen. Nestled in the woods beside a river, it felt like it had been perfectly curated for our enjoyment. The scavenger hunt to find the key, generator, and water controls became a playful exploration. Inside, a small kitchen with an unconventional portable RV toilet greeted us. The oddity of having instructions framed on the wall made me chuckle, but I preferred it to the anxiety of staring into the unknown.

Two futons on the main floor and beds in the loft awaited us, along with other intriguing finds—books, binoculars, and a record player. The cabin was a treasure trove, igniting the excitement of two kids at Disneyland. After unpacking groceries and settling our bags on the futons, we decided to leave the sleeping arrangements for later.

Outside, Kelly practiced yoga while I watched the flowing water from a swing by the river. As I allowed the scenery of the river, trees, and the A-frame to envelop me, I felt transported on a wave of nostalgia that collapsed the years and brought me back to my childhood home. An irresistible urge to sit in the river seized me. I loved the invigorating feel of icy water, but another motive lurked. It was a desire to strip down to my underwear and bra—to impress Kelly, I realized.

I had engaged in countless peculiarities to impress men, but this confounded me. Rather than dissecting the puzzling inclination, I chose to let it be. Kelly joined me on the swing, sitting close. The desire to hold her hand, strange as it was, surfaced. I acknowledged it without overanalyzing, feeling like an observer rather than the protagonist. Perhaps the residual high from our newfound friendship or the exclusive one-on-one time fueled this strangeness. Regardless, the moment felt surreal, transcending time and the outside world. I wished that we could linger indefinitely in our sanctuary, sensing some inexplicable connection—to the place, to Kelly, or to both at once.

Kelly treated me to dinner, and I felt like a rockstar. The realization that a celebrity chef was preparing a private meal for me in a secluded cabin heightened the coolness factor. Amid my enthusiastic consumption of the delicious food she prepared, I noticed Kelly was abstaining from eating. Anxiety crept in. *Am I eating too fast? Should I wait for something? Does she regret being here?* My mind raced with self-doubt, and I convinced myself that Kelly wanted to go home. The prospect of her wanting to leave unnerved me. I grappled with insecurities, my peace and contentment at odds with my nervous state. It was an inexplicable evening that ranked among the best in my life, yet there was still so much dissonance inside me.

Darkness descended with a myriad of stars before we realized it. We went in the cabin and played records I selected, their sounds a seamless complement to each moment. Unlike my usual bedtime contemplations, yearning for an escape that wouldn't cause offense, I was immersed in my conversation with Kelly and gripped by a desire to stay awake all night. Lost in dialogue with Kelly, the time simply seemed to face away. We opted to sleep on the futons downstairs, unfolding them with the finesse of seasoned futon owners. Though blankets were scarce, we settled in, discussing various topics in the dark. The pauses in conversation stretched longer into the night, and I hesitated to break it each time, fearing it might disrupt her sleep. I lay there, straining to discern her state—sleeping or awake? The uncertainty rendered me sleepless.

Sometime in the middle of the night, a sound startled me. Panic set in—an unwelcome visitor, a mouse, scampered across the floor. I loathed mice, so my fear quickly escalated to irrational heights. I contemplated waking Kelly, since the notion of facing this mouse alone unnerved me. It was a dilemma: reveal my irrational fear or maintain a facade of composure? My attempt at waking her with a loud cough failed, and crossing the floor with a mouse as my unwanted companion felt unthinkable, so my internal debate raged on. I yearned to talk to her, to share the burden of the mouse dragon with her. I felt overcome with a desire to crawl into her bed.

Morning arrived, and with minimal sleep, I eagerly anticipated a cozy morning with Kelly and a cup of tea. She finally woke up on her own, my attempts to subtly rouse her proving futile. I made tea for both of us, and we braved the chilly weather on the swing. It was a pleasant, albeit freezing, experience. Back inside, we huddled in our sleeping bags, delving into conversations about marriage, life, dreams, and everything in between. Kelly, after a few minutes, asked if she could join me on my futon. My response—enthusiastic and perhaps too loud—revealed the longing I felt. It was a remarkable moment. We were sitting close but not touching, exploring each other and being explored with our words. The depth seemed endless, and I wondered how I could have known Kelly for so long without ever talking like this before.

The morning passed slowly, full of our seamless conversation, until we reluctantly packed up and bid farewell to the cabin. A somber energy enveloped us, and a sense of sadness accompanied our departure. With no more excuses to delay, we loaded the car and set out. Kelly's afternoon flight loomed, and we decided on lunch in Boulder before heading to the airport. The heaviness intensified as we neared our destination as a weight that settled in my chest, unarticulated but palpable.

Chapter 15

Five-Finger Fit

As we approached the last turn into the airport, I was seized by an overwhelming darkness. I felt profoundly alone, sad, and almost hopeless. Soon, and without warning, tears were streaming down my face—though "tears streamed down my face" doesn't really do it justice. That sounds more like a few tears trickled out, or that my feelings came up slowly or with some warning. Nope.

I burst into tears, going from driving along and minding my own business to full-on ugly crying and having a complete meltdown. I had no idea what was going on, as it had never happened to me before. I never had the tears come so quickly or so hard without first identifying the feeling that was causing them. The realization always came first—a thought about loneliness, sadness, loss, or regret—so what did it mean when the tears came first? I wasn't even sure what I was crying about or why I was crying so hard, and all in front of Kelly!

Kelly stared at me with such a sense of knowing. I felt so self-conscious, but I couldn't pull it together. I couldn't stop crying, so I couldn't even say anything, and I was so overcome by my emotions that I could hardly even feel embarrassed. I kept trying to take control of the situation, yet every time I did, a new set of sobs enveloped me. I felt like I should explain myself or at least say something, but it seemed like she knew more of what was going on than I did. So, I simply drove and sobbed.

After the initial bout of gut-level crying, I took an assessment. I tried to ask myself what I was feeling. Though I didn't know immediately, I dug. This was deeper than sadness. It was grief. After over a decade of inner and spiritual work, it wasn't often that I was at a loss about my own emotions, but this one was taking me for a ride.

I went inward and processed out loud the best I could. "I have no idea what's going on. The best I can explain it is that I love my life. I love ministry and feel such a deep sense of purpose serving. I also love where I live; I love my home at the parsonage and have a great community in Colorado. I love my life and yet feel a deep sense of grief at dropping you off at the airport. It's like I'm about to say goodbye to the best part of my life. And I have no idea what I'm saying right now."

I turned to see Kelly looking over at me with such loving compassion. "I think I might know what's going on," she said.

Well, that makes one of us, I thought. How could she know when I was at such a loss? This was so bizarre and unsettling.

"Molly," she continued, "this is what happened to me when I dropped you off at the airport in Nashville."

Everything around us seemed to freeze. The car was moving —the airport looming—but we weren't. I was frozen as my mind rushed to catch up with this information. *Kelly feels this too? She's been feeling this for weeks?* My mind raced as it tried to fill in the gaps with this new information.

"That's why I flew back out here," she continued. "That's why I was crying the other morning."

I replayed the tape of the last couple weeks in my mind, adding her words to the narrative. *That was why Kelly invited me to the concert and wanted to spend one-on-one time with me,* I thought. *That was why she was crying in the other room with Jenna.* It had bothered me that Kelly hadn't come to me, but now it made sense. She couldn't confide in me or talk to me because she was crying *about* me. I felt a flood of relief.

However, my relief was short-lived and was immediately replaced with confusion. Everything went cloudy again in my mind. I finally managed to ask aloud, "What does this mean?"

"I have no idea," Kelly said. "I came back to Colorado to find out. Like I said yesterday, Molly, I think you're my person," she finally said, calmly and quietly. There was such softness and sweetness about her. I felt myself melt in the car beside her.

"Yeah, I think maybe you are my person." As the words left my mouth, I knew they weren't accurate. It was all becoming clear, as though I had turned a radio dial until I no longer heard static. I didn't *think* Kelly was my person. This time, I was certain.

I was surprised at my level of knowing. The information seemed so out of left field and so disorienting to everything I knew, but it also rang so true. There weren't many things I knew for sure, but I was absolutely certain of this.

My mind went back to *Grey's Anatomy*. *What are we? Are we best friends now? Hold on. Is it more than that?* The sensations and emotions I was experiencing felt brand new—I was excited, relieved, confused, and yet so peaceful at the same time. I couldn't understand it, and yet, it made perfect sense. How could I be bewildered and comforted at the same time? What was this calm coming over me in the midst of my anxieties? It felt like I had finally found a precious item that I had been sick over losing, or that my medical results had come back clear after anticipating the worst. I had been holding so much tension in this pit in my stomach forever and was only just realizing that it was beginning to ease.

"I need to pull over," I said. All the emotions were catching up to me, and driving 70 miles an hour didn't seem like the best idea. We rode in silence as I found my way to the airport's cell phone lot. I looked at the monitors and saw that we still had time before Kelly's flight, and I felt a rush of relief. This, I imagined, was the conversation we'd been trying to have for the last few days. Here it was, coming out all at once, and I was struggling to keep up. My heart and soul were finally in the driver's seat and, after trying to call all the shots for most of my life, my mind was a mess as it tried to catch up.

It felt better to lean into my heart instead of my brain, but it was also disorienting. My mind had always been the one navigating, but it had always been clumsy, not knowing exactly where to go and never pausing to find the correct turn. Now that my heart was driving, it was like it knew exactly where to go. Things suddenly felt effortless and smooth, and now my mind was reeling as it tried to make meaning out of everything. *If I can lean into my heart*, I thought, *maybe I can just sit back and relax a little.*

I parked the car and turned to Kelly, finally able to look her in the eyes. We were both crying a bit. She looked different, as if I had never really seen her before, and now, she was coming into focus. Her features and expression felt familiar on a deep level.

I don't recall our exact words, but I remember contemplating what life would be like now that I had a person. As we talked, Kelly started crying harder, saying she didn't know if she could upheave her life to be with me.

Part of me understood exactly what she meant. She felt like I was her person, a life partner, not just a friend. Even though I had never articulated this possibility, in my heart, I agreed. I could envision my life with her.

My mind protested, *Are we talking about being in love with each other? I'm straight. Wait... am I straight? Am I gay? Am I in love with Kelly?*

I remembered the night before, in and out of sleep and wishing all the while that I could snuggle up next to her. I remembered wanting to hold her hand in the swing. I remembered wanted to get in the river. My mind was reeling, but my heart was leading, so at peace with a divine knowing. With that knowing came even more questions. *What does it mean to be gay? What will the church think? Am I crossing a line? Can I do this? Can I do this? Can I do this?*

Yes, I can do this!

I heard Kelly as if she were far away, as if her voice were coming through water, as she talked about upending her whole life so we could be together. *What if we could have both?* I tried to rationalize *What if it could be an "and" and not an "or"?*

"Maybe this is like Meredith and Cristina," I said finally. "Could you be my person and stay married to your husband?" Even as I made this suggestion, I was still trying to catch up with how what I *felt* was so at odds with what I *thought*.

"No, I don't think I could do that," she said calmly. I completely agreed.

"Yeah, I think so too," I replied. "I think you are my person." I was repeating myself both to ground this new reality and to catch up with this sudden revelation. As the saying goes, there are things that we know we know: I know about preaching, as well as how to do it. And then, there are things that we know we don't know: I know *about* heart surgery but I have no idea how to do it. Most of what we "know" is just stuff we're aware of, not things that we understand.

A dam burst between my brain and my soul. What I knew in that moment flooded together with what I didn't understand. I knew I loved Kelly in a way that I'd never loved anyone before —I *knew* it. But I'd never considered being with a woman before. I'd never even thought to consider it.

"You're my person," I anchored again.

"Yes, I'm your person," she echoed.

"You're my person, and not just as a friend," I confirmed. The knowing was clear, but the logistics were a mind fuck. *Kelly is married. Kelly isn't just married; she's been married for twenty years. She's the definition of loyalty and family. And I am her pastor!* My brain was taking over again, and I suddenly seized with this realization. She had been a member of the church I was currently serving. *Oh shit.* Was I in trouble? Had I crossed a line or abused my power in some way?

I suddenly felt sick. "I need to call the bishop," I blurted. Yes! That sounded like something to grasp onto, an action I could take. I needed to call the bishop. I needed some help navigating this tornado that had just swept through my understanding of myself.

I felt equal parts exhilarated, confused, terrified, and calm, expecting myself to freak out at any moment. This was way out of control and so out of my comfort zone. In the span of about 30 minutes, I had gone from talking to a newfound best friend to considering she might be my life partner. A process like this should take years, and in all my past attempts, I had never even gotten to that elusive, 100-percent-sure feeling. I questioned myself so much in relationships, but this felt so different—I just *knew*. There was nothing to question, only details to sort out.

I felt almost like an observer of my own life in that parking lot. I could hear myself saying things with such peace and certainty. Part of me felt so calm, but my mind was doing gymnastics, insisting I should be freaking out. *We are talking about starting a new relationship here!* Backflip. *I'm in the middle of a nasty—capital-N nasty—divorce.* Handstand. *I*

thought I would never do this again, and certainly not this soon.
Cartwheel. *Kelly is a woman. I'm a woman!* Somersault. But
even that last thought didn't cause a blip on the radar of my
heart—*No big deal*, it insisted calmly in response.

It's strange to me now that this didn't create more of a panic.
My thoughts were running in circles, my brain trying to label
what was happening and put me into some kind of box. *What
does this mean? Am I a lesbian? Am I bisexual? Will I need to
come out?* My brain blathered these and a thousand other questions between leaps and handsprings, but they were muffled by
my heart, by my calm, confident knowing. This just felt right,
despite the fact it was so far from who I had known myself to be.

This would also mean so much upheaval in my life. *Would I
need to move? Would I have to give up ministry? What would
my church think? My family? My friends?* Everything I had built
was suddenly in question, and I was strangely okay with that.
But what would this mean for Kelly? I actually really liked her
husband and had huge respect for him. I considered him a good
friend and would never, ever want to hurt him or cause him any
pain. And how would this affect Lucy? I'd always felt a special
connection to her, and now I wondered if there had been something deeper all along. She was such a cool kid, and although I
delighted at the chance to be closer to her, I also felt sick about
tearing her family apart. I didn't want to do anything that wasn't
honest or above board. And yet, I still knew and felt a peace I
had never known before.

With a million logistical details separating us and a thousand ways this would upend so many lives, there was a stillness

and acceptance about what was opening between us. I hadn't felt this before. This wasn't something I was trying to get, achieve, or accumulate. What was happening between Kelly and me didn't feel transactional the way all my previous relationships had. This felt like a gift, something I had received without having to ask or earn. This wasn't an exchange; I didn't have to give up who I was for this. Instead, there was surprise, delight, gratitude, and receiving.

I had been praying for a person, a life partner, a lover since the seventh grade. I had written this desire down and put it in a special prayer box. I had blown out birthday candles for this wish. I had pleaded, even wailed in desperate loneliness. I'd created vision boards and set intentions and visualized ideal scenes. In a million different ways, I had asked the universe for a person to do life with, someone who could really see me, who got me, and who would love me back just as I was, and here it was—here *she* was.

Here was this gift before me, but my mind felt so afraid to open it, lean into it, or even trust it. My heart knew, but my brain wanted to proceed with caution. I didn't want to mess this up like I had so many times before. I wanted to choose each word with intention and care. I wanted each step to be made with love and kindness for all involved. This was all so new.

In the past, I'd followed my lust or craving for validation or acceptance like an addiction, without weighing how my actions might impact or even hurt other people. It was about me before, and now, despite how strongly I felt, I needed to be patient. I didn't need to be in a hurry, and I wanted to move forward in a way that was kind and loving for everyone.

I put my hand on Kelly's leg, hoping the gesture would show her that I saw her that I felt it, too. I felt what she was feeling, and I wanted to do this thing with her, together. She immediately grabbed my hand and and her fingers locked into mine in a beyond-perfect fit.

Before that moment, my relationships had been what I call a "two- or three-finger fit." Each time, something hadn't lined up or connected just right. Until that day at the airport, I had accepted that a three-finger fit was the best I could, so it had to be good enough. I had been willing to do the hard work and effort that the three-finger-fit kind of connection required, but a profound amount of energy goes into holding onto something that isn't right.

But now, in the parking lot, just like that, I had found an effortless five-finger fit. Kelly's hand just fit into mine, and it felt better than anything I'd experienced before—better than any hug, smile, or even any orgasm.

This was connection. *This* was comfort. *This* was home.

Chapter 16

Pain and Purpose

I could have held Kelly's hand forever, but I knew it wasn't time. As much as I wanted to hold onto her, I took my hand away. I wanted to do this right. I wanted to be respectful, and things needed to happen before I did anything. I needed to talk to the bishop. I needed Kelly to be free to be with me. If this was forever, I wanted to make sure we started with integrity, with love. We needed to start clean.

"Can we get a sandwich?" Kelly asked.

This bomb had just dropped, and a million pieces of our lives before the gift of this conversation were projected into the air. I felt enough of a sense of calm and knowing to think, *Okay, what's next?* Obviously, we needed to grab some food now that we had that all taken care of.

"Of course," I replied.

We got out of the car at the cell phone waiting lot. There

was a gas station and a few places to eat nearby. The lot seemed strangely quiet, as if we were the only ones there. Maybe it was the time of day, but we parked right up front and walked into an open atrium of restaurants, restrooms, and vending areas with only a few people milling about. I felt such a high as I held the door open for Kelly. *Is this how teens feel when they have their first boyfriend or girlfriend? Is this what I've been missing —this floating, elated feeling?* I'm sure I had a huge grin as I walked in, side by side with Kelly. Like Christmas morning before opening presents, my anticipation and excitement were overflowing.

As I spotted a Schlotzsky's among the restaurants, I said light-heartedly, "If we ever revisit this conversation, can we playfully dub it the 'Schlotzsky's Incident'?" I glanced at Kelly and noticed a bewildered look on her face, wanting to speak but hesitating.

"Um—we're definitely going to need to discuss this again," she said quickly. I smiled.

Ten minutes later, we were effortlessly sharing a Schlotzsky's sandwich. It may have looked mundane to other people sitting nearby, but it was a monumental moment for Kelly and me. I had never felt more myself, more seen and understood, that I did in that moment, sharing a Schlotzsky's sandwich at the airport.

The sense of ease continued into our light conversation. A few people walked by our table, but it seemed as if we were the only people in the world. Everything about this place screamed highway rest stop: the plastic swivel chairs, the picnic style seats, the vending machines, and banks of restrooms. But it felt magical to me.

We finished our food and casually made our way back to the car, and I drove us the short distance to the departure lane, pulling up next to the curb. As I got out to help Kelly with her bag, a deep peace settled within me. Other travelers bustled around the drop-off area, juggling suitcases and boarding passes and saying their farewells. I gave Kelly a lingering hug and said goodbye. It didn't feel like a painful parting, nor did it carry the weight of all the emotions we had just discussed. I smiled, waved, and said simply, "See ya."

She smiled back with tears in her eyes, then walked inside.

As I got back in the car and pulled away from the curb, I wondered, *Did that really just happen?* My mind grappled with the enormity of the situation, and I wasn't quite ready to comprehend the magnitude of the whirlwind that had just been unleashed. Driving away from the airport, I took a few moments to bask in the peace and gratitude of this profound gift. If all I had were those few minutes of holding Kelly's hand, it would be more than I ever thought possible. I had touched the real thing. I had finally found what I was looking for.

As I drove the two hours home, I waited with anticipation for the perfect song to come on the radio. Many had come close, but none had yet nailed the feeling that matched mine. Was there even a song out there that could capture the intensity and mix of my emotions? As I was contemplating, the song came on. It wasn't one I expected or thought would be a fit for this moment, but the more I listened, the more it made sense. I smiled as the familiar tune flooded my ears. As Johnny Nash's voice poured from the speakers, it felt like the universe's way of acknowledging this moment of clarity.

I can make it now, the pain is gone
All of the bad feelings have disappeared
Here is that rainbow I've been praying for

As I listened to the lyrics, amid all the recent memories of Kelly clamoring for attention, an older one surfaced, one from way back. I could vividly recall a moment from my middle school days, sitting alone on the top bleachers in the gym during an assembly. A man with long blond hair and a guitar had captured my attention, sharing a story with an unexpected twist that left an indelible mark on my soul. He told the school that a drinking game gone awry had resulted in the tragic death of his friend due to alcohol poisoning.

His story, raw and unadorned, had cut through the air and left a profound impact on me. It wasn't the cautionary tale about binge-drinking that resonated; it was the awakening of a desire to become a speaker, to have a story that could evoke emotions and inspire change. My dream, ignited that day during that assembly before lying dormant for two decades, had resurfaced again when I was 35 years old, during a critical moment of crisis in my life. I had found myself facing a suicidal crisis, and remembered that middle school assembly that had lit a spark within me. In the depths of my despair, a new trajectory for my life emerged. I decided to write a book, share my story, and embark on a journey of speaking engagements.

I dove headfirst into realizing my dream, writing my first book and passionately sharing my story with anyone who would listen. Even though it was scary, and even though I didn't understand how it would all work out, something about it felt right. Something about writing and speaking *fit*. That dream of being a speaker, which I eventually thought had faded away, resurrected itself again with renewed vigor as I grappled with the complexities of ministry—and now, the dream loomed large once again. The details weren't clear, but the feeling was right.

Reality infiltrated my euphoria on the mountainous journey home. Amid all my concerns about embracing love, coming out, and navigating the intricacies of my new relationship, telling the bishop emerged as my primary worry. The church, a newfound cornerstone in my life, had unexpectedly become my paramount concern. Reflecting on my faith journey, I realized the profound impact it had had on my priorities.

In the tumultuous journey of my life, where shadows threatened every dawn, I had discovered the transformative power of faith in darkness. The same journey that led me from the precipice of despair had also propelled me toward ministry, a profound calling that involved weaving threads of pain, healing, and divine guidance into a rich tapestry.

My plea to the divine, to spirit, to God, resonated through years of silent struggles with depression and suicidal thoughts. Soon, a daily prayer kept escaping my lips: a desperate request to find a reason to embrace each new morning. This whispered cry unknowingly set the stage for a profound transformation that entering the ministry would bring.

During this time, a courageous confession shattered the walls of shame surrounding my battles. When I first uttered the words, "I think about killing myself all the time," they became the catalyst for a healing journey that spanned over a decade. With a clinical diagnosis, a master's degree in spiritual psychology, and the beginnings of newfound self-love, I started to emerge from the shadows.

This evolution led me to advocacy, particularly in suicide prevention. Immersed in training, sharing my story nationwide, and combating the stigma surrounding mental health, I sensed this was just the beginning of a grander calling. A pivot occurred when I witnessed the heartbreaking prevalence of suicidal ideation among young children, especially in elementary schools. Years spent honing suicide intervention skills and becoming a go-to for crisis support unfolded into a role focused on prevention.

Elementary schools were my imperative battleground. I co-created a program for fifth graders blending basic suicide prevention with social-emotional learning. The shocking stories of kids' despair, like a second-grader attempting suicide with a gym rope, fueled my resolve. I grappled with a choice: should I continue my work on perfecting intervention or pivot to addressing root causes upstream? Ministry unexpectedly emerged as the answer.

This divine summons shocked me. Without a religious upbringing, I had resisted religion for most of my life. Pursuing a master's of divinity and eventually becoming the senior pastor at UMC of Eagle Valley had brought an unforeseen sense of purpose. This calling, despite its initial strangeness, fit surprisingly well.

Seeds of that call to ministry had been planted during my darkest hours. At 35 and contemplating suicide, I had unintentionally embarked on a journey of self-discovery. Seeking to understand myself had led to an unexpected conversation with the divine, guiding me toward what I eventually realized was my purpose.

In the rearview mirror, the airport faded behind me on a road laden with twists and turns. The mountainous terrain ahead, like the journey of my life, was still veiled in mystery. The whispers of my initial, incomprehensible, divine call were still with me, intertwining with new realizations of pain and purpose. As the wheels rolled on, I pondered the unexpected intersection of ministry and my deepest struggles. Little did I know that this path, marked by faith and resilience, would lead me to confront my most pressing, current concern—the church.

In the quiet hum of the car, I sensed the anticipation of challenges to come, the delicate balance between faith and expectations. The very institution that had become my worry, my unexpected priority, now stood on the horizon of change. The road home was not just a physical journey but a symbolic one, a prelude to a future where faith would be tested, boundaries redefined, and my path to ministry unraveled.

As I traveled the interstate, the car ride became a space for my mind to dance and play with the myriad memories of the past twenty-four hours. I relived the excitement and confusion of affirming our connection, feeling the warmth of Kelly's hand in mine and savoring our final hug at the airport.

* * *

When I arrived home after picking Otis up at doggy daycare, I walked into the clean and orderly house, just as I left it, but it all felt vastly different. Suddenly, the organization didn't seem quite so important. I felt more detached from needing the house to be just right, because I felt more "right" internally. I was startled by the buzzing of my phone. It was a text from Kelly, a simple yet poignant message:

Boarding now. Miss you.

My heart raced as a wave of emotions crashed over me. *When will I see her again?* I thought. *How will this unfold?* The questions multiplied, but the feelings were crystal clear—love, longing, and a profound sense of connection. I replied:

Safe travels. Miss you too... a lot.

The floodgates of emotions opened once again, and I found myself sobbing, the intensity of the rollercoaster ride finally catching up with me. I stumbled to my bedroom, seeking the familiar paths of the parsonage through a curtain of tears. Were they tears of sadness, longing, or joy? The boundaries blurred, and I lay on my bed, feeling the softness of the comforter against my face. Still rejoicing in seeing me after a few days, Otis desperately licked away my salty tears, comforting me. The tears had a life of their own, a release of the overwhelming emotions that had built up during the drive home.

Before I let myself go too far, I knew I needed to clear this with the church. I knew that in my role as a pastor, I held great responsibility, and doing any harm was the last thing I wanted. My first call was to the district superintendent, my most immediate boss in the church, so I punched in her number. I always felt a bit nervous talking to her, but now, the stakes were higher. I wanted her support, but more than anything, I wanted to know I could pursue a relationship with Kelly as a senior pastor. What were the rules for pastors dating?

As I clumsily came out for the first time and shared that I was in love with a woman, she responded with nothing but excitement and support. She kept reminding me that this was good news, I hadn't crossed any lines, and that I should enjoy this gift! The light was green; I could do this thing.

The district superintendent suggested that I call the bishop for support. I was so new to the world of coming out that I didn't even know what I didn't know. Of course, support would be great!

A few things were high on my list of topics I wanted to know more about. One, how could I not know I was gay? This seemed like something I should be aware of, so how was I so blind to it? And second, why did I feel like a teenager—giddy, full of brain fog, and constantly devouring sugar?

If I was a little nervous talking to the district superintendent, I was exponentially more nervous to talk to the bishop.
She was such a big deal. But the second I heard her voice, I felt
more reassured than ever before. Any doubt or fear I harbored
since leaving that airport parking lot was eased. She guided me
in a way that helped me see everything that I already knew but
was just beyond my understanding. She was a true leader, for
sure. Not only did I have her support, but I felt spiritually
guided in a deep and profound way. I felt more seen, heard, and
understood than ever before. It was intoxicating to not only be
seen for my truest self, but fully accepted.

Now, this, I thought, *is heaven on earth.*

After the emotional purge, I rose from my bed where I had
been snuggled up tight with Otis, my phone a beacon of connection in my pocket. The idea of dinner felt foreign—frozen pizza
or peanut butter and jelly sounded tasteless in the face of the
emotional storm. The cascade of emotions, words, and thoughts
yearned for expression.

I walked into my office, its familiarity and silence a comfort.
I glanced at the row of journals on the shelf, each a repository of
my thoughts and dreams. I selected a new, limited-edition Mole-
skin journal with "I Solemnly Swear" embossed on the cover, a
fitting sentiment for the intensity of my feelings. The plastic
wrap crackled as I peeled it off, revealing pristine pages
untouched by anyone else.

In the quiet of my office, with the fresh journal and my
favorite pen in hand, I let the words flow. *Hello, my darling,* I
wrote on the first page in blue ink, dating it September 3. The

ink on the pages mirrored the inkling of emotions that had surfaced during the drive. My written words became a channel for the unspoken, a sanctuary for the cacophony of emotions swirling within me.

Did I just fall in love with you? Did I just find my person? Did the rest of my life just open up? Did I just fall in love with a woman? Did I just say it out loud?

The pages unfolded as a love letter, a raw outpouring of desires, dreams, and a willingness to embrace the messiness of love.

I want to hold your hand. I want to hug you. I want to lay in bed and hold you. I want you to wake me up when you can't sleep. I want you to cry in my arms. I want all that and more. I want to explore all this with you. I want to discover your body as I have your heart and your mind.

The ink flowed freely, capturing the essence of a newfound connection and the possibilities that danced in my mind. Dreams of attending a Broncos game together, exploring bookstores across the States, or simply snuggling up together to watch a Christmas movie took shape on the pages. Amid the euphoria, a shadow loomed—the realization of an ocean of commitment, family, vows, and the delicate balance of love and respect.

*How can I just want love and fully share it all and feel
like in doing so I would be destroying something? I'm so
conflicted. I don't want to dishonor your marriage. I
don't want to disappoint the church. Why does this
blessing seem to come with such a heavy cost?*

The pen in my hand became a conduit for patience and an acknowledgment that love unfolds in its own time.

*For me, this (us) isn't a yes or no, it's a when. I will be
patient for love to work itself out. I will wait. It will be
clear when it is our time. And I promise you, I will not
run. I'll be right here waiting, my darling.*

The ink dried on the pages, leaving behind a testament to the vulnerability, passion, and uncertainty that love had unfurled within me. As I closed the journal, the weight of the words settled, and I sought refuge in the respite of sleep, eager to see what the dawn would bring.

Chapter 17

It Must Have Been Love

Finding my person wasn't the fairy tale I had envisioned. I thought everything would magically fall into place just like it does in books and movies, but I was experiencing the opposite—utter wreckage. I had prayed for this my entire life, often thinking that maybe, finally, I had earned it. When things with Kelly had become clear, I began realizing that *earning* wasn't at the core of it, that it wasn't about being good enough. This was a difficult model to shed. I needed to accept a female partner, and yet so many of my core foundational beliefs stood in the way. This love was everything I ever wanted, but it came with complexities—I had found the love of my life, but she was married. Just as I was about to get everything I ever wanted, I felt it was all about to crumble.

A few days after our wild car conversation, Kelly texted:

Can we talk on the phone soon?

We felt the same way: this was something extraordinary. However, the looming shadows of her husband and the potential fallout in my professional life made me sick with worry. Our love was stronger than the challenges—I was certain.

Describing this as the love of a lifetime felt cliché, and it was unmistakably that—but it was also paired with a knowing so clear it was like a light switch had flipped on. Love, for me, had always been a mental exercise fueled by low self-esteem and chasing the illusion of acceptance and belonging. I thought finding a partner was the key to belonging, but my relationships had always pulled me further away from it. Kelly was different. *We* were different. What we had wasn't about proving or earning; it was a recognition, a deep knowing. It wasn't a choice; it was a must, an unstoppable force. Before, I had experienced love as *getting*. Now, it felt more like *being*.

Over the course of many text messages and calls, we eventually decided it was time for Kelly to tell her husband, and I grew more and more anxious. I knew the pain she was about to inflict because I had been there myself, asking for a divorce from a loving man. I felt it all: the guilt Kelly must have felt for having this conversation, the pain of Rick losing his marriage, the heartache for Lucy of her family breaking up. There was so much loss in all of this, and I felt responsible. I was doing this, wasn't I? I knew in my heart this was good, but the weight of my responsibility for the heartache that would result from it felt impossible to hold.

And it *was* impossible. It was impossible to continue down the path of being who I had always been. I had always chosen the "right" thing, followed the rules, and gone with the flow. I evaluated and navigated everyone else's feelings before making a decision. This choice was going to hurt people, that was clear, but this time was different. The person I was willing to disappoint wasn't me. This was new, and things inside of me began to shift with this decision. Parts of me I had long forgotten were waking up.

It was yet another Wednesday morning, but nothing was typical about it. I was in my office at the parsonage with a Bible and notebook splayed out on my desk as I began to work on the sermon for Sunday when the text came in:

I'm meeting with Rick today.

My stomach constricted and my breath caught. I dropped my pen and immediately typed a response:

Oh my goodness. Are you okay?

Perched on the edge of my seat—literally—I waited for the three dots to turn into words. I tapped my leg so fast that my heart rate skyrocketed like I was running in my chair. She wrote back:

I don't know.

I ached for her. *Oh, my love,* I thought. *What should I do? Should I get on a plane and fly out there to be with her? Is that the totally right or wrong thing to do?* The physical distance was so great that it felt like a chasm. Without her, I felt so lost. I typed back:

I'm here.

I wished there was more I could say, because it didn't like nearly enough.

Knowing the conversation between Kelly and Rick was happening, I couldn't think of anything else. Time seemed to stand still. *What is happening? Has she told him? How did it go? Did she go through with it? What if she changes her mind?* I felt an overwhelming sense of helplessness. All I could do was wait, paralyzed in the darkness of not knowing. My stomach churning, I decided that I couldn't stand sitting at my desk any longer and paced into my bedroom.

I sat on the edge of the bed in my dark room, holding my phone, waiting. The waiting game was maddening, and the anxiety was taking its toll. At one point, Jenna reached out and let me know that she'd heard from Kelly—she'd told Rick but wasn't able to talk to me yet. I finally couldn't stand it anymore, so I responded, desperate for a lifeline:

Is she okay?

After a moment, Jenna responded:

No.

One agonizing hour later, I received a cryptic heart emoji from Kelly and confusion and fear set in. Desperation led me to send more texts as I aimlessly wandered the house, seeking reassurance. I crawled into the bathtub, all my clothes still on, and just sat there. I stared at the heart emoji as I awaited a reply to my messages. *What does it mean? Is this a sign of "I'm with you," or is this a heartfelt goodbye?*

I thought maybe some music would help, and I hit shuffle on iTunes. "It must have been love, but it's over now... It must have been good, but I lost it somehow," Roxette crooned. The tinny music from my phone echoed off the bathroom walls. *Seriously?* I felt immediate separation, pain, longing. It was over before it even began. The lyrics resonated, capturing the pain of losing something that felt irreplaceable. I began to cry, then sob. I cried so desperately I imagined my tears filling the tub. My heart ached in a way I didn't know was possible.

In despair, I eventually sought comfort in my bed, its softness a balm for my wounded soul. As I fell asleep, I clung to the hope that the love I felt was not lost. I sent one last, simple text to Kelly that evening:

What do you need?

There was no reply, and the next morning also brought no

relief. I drifted purposelessly through the house all day, not even realizing where I was going or what I was doing. Eventually, as evening sharpened the light pouring in through the windows, a simple response from Kelly changed everything:

You.

This single word breathed life back into me, and the hope for our love burned brighter than ever. It must have been love, but it was *not* over now—not even by a long shot.

Chapter 18

From Tomboy to Sexy

Stepping off the emotional roller coaster, I still felt the lingering wobbliness from the tumultuous ride of the previous day. The spectrum of my emotions had ranged from gripping fear, preceding Kelly's crucial conversation with Rick, to a deep well of grief, when I thought I had lost her. Finally, I had soared to the heights of elation as I realized she had chosen me. When it came, the revelation hit hard: Kelly was officially separated from her husband.

In the aftermath, relief coexisted with pain, sadness, and every conceivable emotion in between. While the specifics of Kelly's conversation with Rick remained veiled, its brutal impact on both sides was palpable. Rick, devastated and heartbroken, was left reeling, while Kelly grappled with profound pangs of loss, guilt, and a haunting sense of failure. The foundations of her beliefs about loyalty, love, family, and self were shaken to the core. Her devastation became tangible, and my heart ached as I witnessed her questioning everything she held dear. In a surprising twist, I found myself not just empathizing but feeling the weight of her grief and sadness myself. My poor girl, so torn, so shattered and hurting. In the silent, lonely moments before sleep, her brokenness enveloped me each night as I lay in bed. Empathy, a gift and a challenge, allowed me to feel her core-level pain and loss. Despite the joy and connection between us, an undercurrent of her unexpected separation lingered, casting shadows on the profound love blossoming between us.

One such night, while I lay in bed hoping for sleep but knowing it would elude me for at least another hour, "Chasing Cars" by Snow Patrol played softly in the background. Its lyrics encapsulated the essence of how I felt and how I knew Kelly must've felt so often during our long days of separateness and pain: "Would you lie with me and just forget the world?"

I did just that: I lay there with her.

Although physically separated, as I thought of her and held her, almost in a meditative state, I could actually feel her. It was like nothing I'd ever experienced—she might as well have been right next to me. Although it was only our souls connecting, it felt physical, emotional, and intimate. This was new, an experience that expanded what I knew to be possible in the world of connection and belonging. My limited views were starting to shatter as I continued to bust the ceiling on my understanding of love.

The next dawn brought the routine of checking my phone

for her messages, and I found one she had sent earlier that morning:

I hope I don't wake you. But I can't stand not connecting when I wake.

A seamless connection was foreshadowed in that message, and it unfolded in the days that followed, transcending the limitations of time, space, and verbal communication. It was as if our hearts and minds were entangled, dancing to a rhythm that defied explanation. In the realm of soul connections, the dance extends beyond the physical and mental. Our journey unfolded as a cascade of emotions, a language that surpassed words. Conversations with Kelly were not mere exchanges of information; they were heart-to-heart dialogues.

The revelation that we were so deeply connected despite our separate locations and difficulties came not in the grand gestures but in the quiet moments, the vulnerabilities shared. The messiness of life, the complexities that might daunt others, became the canvas for our shared art. Facing challenges head-on, we discovered the alchemical magic hidden within the chaos.

In those days of navigating what would come next, I began to look back and question everything I had known to be true about intimate relationships. Things were revealing themselves to be not what they seemed. One aspect of relationships that had always seemed to elude me was the idea of being sexy. For years, to me, feeling sexy seemed like the Mount

Everest of self-love. And I was starting all the way at the bottom.

When I had hit suicidal crisis at 35, I'd been struggling with depression for decades, and I was exhausted. Without hope or a will to go on, I made a plan to end my life. Instead of ending my life, my suicide attempt had ended the season of my life without faith and purpose. In the moments leading up to my plan, I had a profound spiritual awakening. Maybe it was the still, small voice of God or some other divine intervention, or maybe it was my own deeper knowing speaking. I don't know, but the message was clear: "Molly, what if you lived your life for *you*?"

I was shocked. What was this voice? What did it mean? And I was curious. I was certainly going to check it out before killing myself. This began my journey of self-exploration. What would living my life for myself even look like? I'd been following the rules, conforming, pleasing, and going with the flow of others my entire life. I didn't even know what my own flow would look like.

In that time of healing, I began to recreate my relationship with myself. It was beyond strained by then. I hated myself and loathed the way I looked in the mirror. I found my image disgusting and had a long way to go to climb this mountain. This journey toward self-love, an arduous path for sure, transformed my perception of myself. Years of looking at myself in the mirror every single day would eventually shift the narrative from self-loathing to self-adoration. The morning affirmations would become a celebration of my unique features, a declaration of self-love that resonated beyond the surface. I would transform from disgusting to neutral to lovely.

After years of working on it, I got to a place of recognizing beauty in myself. I began to celebrate the way I looked and enjoyed most pictures taken of me. Rather than cringe, I'd think to myself, *Damn, I look good!* and really believe it. Yet, the concept of "sexy" continued to elude me. *Sexy*—confined to societal definitions of long legs, lipstick, and tight clothes—felt like a straitjacket. My inability to conform haunted me, making every attempt at sexiness feel like enduring a soul injury.

The turning point came in my interactions with Kelly. When I interacted with her, something in me felt different, and I could feel that things were shifting.

One day, she texted me a photo of her wearing a pair of lacy black underwear. She used a few of her fingers to lightly pull up her shirt. I could see the curve of her hips, her abdomen, and the lace. This was my undoing, in so many ways. The moment the text arrived, I felt the exhilaration of connection. It was a rush, a spark across the miles of distance between us. But with the excitement crashed a wave of realization—how could I reciprocate? These were *sexy* underwear, and for all my trying over the years, I didn't know how to be sexy. The sinking feeling in my heart wasn't about the underwear; it was the fear of disappointing the one person I never wanted to let down.

My emotions swung like a pendulum, from the high of connection to the devastating low of perceived failure. My inability to play the game of sexy hit hard, and I questioned my worth and capability. Tears flowed, representing not just the underwear crisis but a lifetime of feeling inadequate in the realm of societal expectations around gender expression. Rather than reply, I retreated to my bed, the repressed pain of decades surfacing, overwhelming and suffocating.

It was a cathartic release, a torrent of suppressed emotions pouring out, and fear crept into the mix—had I opened Pandora's box? My empathic connection with Kelly deepened as she sensed my distress from afar. She could tell I was hurting without words. Our transcendent connection had exposed me. Finally, vulnerably, I texted her:

I can't stop crying.

She called me immediately. Her response was a lifeline, an assurance that I wasn't alone.

"I could feel your pain as I was putting Lucy to bed," she said into the phone. "I'm here. I've got you."

For over an hour, we connected through tears and words. It was a dance, a sharing of pain and acceptance. The experience was transformative, my first real taste of reciprocal emotional connection. In that sacred space, I began to ponder the nature of our bond, the mysterious force that tied us together.

The next morning when I woke up, an unexpected lightness replaced the heaviness. The weight of unexpressed pain had lifted, leaving me perplexed but relieved. The energy had caught up with my mind, and I understood the necessity of that emotional release. I rolled over and opened my messaging app. I revisited the underwear text, and a surprising flip occurred—my body responded, and I felt a newfound appreciation for Kelly's bold expression.

This breakthrough came with a revelation—I didn't need to conform to societal standards of sexy. Authenticity was the new sexy. My rejection of lacy underwear led to this transformative conversation with Kelly, and her unexpected response shattered my preconceptions. She actually laughed when I confessed that I didn't like wearing lacy underwear, insisting she would never want me to! She wasn't attracted to societal norms; she was drawn to my unique style. She said she liked the way I wore my pants low on my hips, that it was *sexy*. The revelation was both liberating and disorienting. My lifelong belief that my preferences made me undesirable crumbled as Kelly expressed love for the very aspects of myself I had once considered flaws.

The journey of self-discovery continued over time as I questioned the societal norms that had dictated my choices up until this point. Researching, buying, and trying boxers for women felt like stepping into a new world. The purchase was exhilarating, and the moment those boxers met my skin, I felt a surge of confidence. It wasn't just underwear; it was a declaration of self-love. Discarding my old underwear was a practical act, but it was also a symbolic one. Until I found something that fit, I hadn't even realized I could be comfortable.

With newfound freedom, I ventured into my closet. The purge of clothes that didn't resonate with love was cathartic. Each discarded piece represented a compromise, a way I had contorted myself to fit societal expectations. The process unearthed the extent of my self-blindness, realizing how I had chipped away at my authenticity without conscious awareness. Bagging up the pile for the thrift store, I marveled at the ways I had played the game of compromise, policing myself to stay within prescribed lines. The clothes I discarded were not just fabric; they were the shedding of layers that obscured my true self. As I liberated myself from the constraints of societal norms, I glimpsed the person I had been searching for—me.

In this metamorphosis, the revelation wasn't just about embracing my tomboy style; it was about redefining beauty on my terms. The discarded clothes were not just donations; they were offerings to the universe, releasing the old to make space for the authentic, unapologetic me. The journey to self-love continued, and with each liberated choice, I embraced the magic of being loved for who I truly was.

It wasn't until Kelly entered my life that the deep wounds of misunderstanding my beauty, authenticity, desirability, and worth began to heal. I continued to find acceptance and desirability in lesbian circles, a revelation that shattered the illusion of my inherent flaws. There was nothing wrong with me at all. Kelly became my beacon of understanding, guiding me toward self-love, acceptance, and the realization that my authentic expression was not just valid but profoundly beautiful.

I emerged from the shadows, embracing my true self and discovering the strength in authenticity. The journey was arduous, but it was leading me to a place where I no longer sought external validation to define my worth.

* * *

One sunny day, as I was organizing what remained in my closet after the purge, I couldn't help but chuckle at the irony of it all. I could never have known that my journey to "sexy" would lead me to wearing pants so low they practically had their own area code, or that the epitome of my tomboy-chic style would be rocking a hoodie like I was about to drop the hottest mixtape of the century. It turns out, my sexy isn't fancy dresses or high heels, it's the low-slung swagger of my pants and the nonchalant comfort of a well-worn sweatshirt. A pair of camouflage-print Converse shoes would've fit right in. Apparently, "sexy" was a state of mind, and fashion could be hilarious.

Baggy shorts, oversized pockets, an unbuttoned shirt—all the things I thought were the antithesis of sexy—became my sexy. In embracing my true self, I discovered that feeling sexy wasn't about conforming to external expectations; it was an internal flame that ignited when I fully embraced and loved myself. Kelly was showing me that the things I thought were most objectionable about my myself were actually the very things she was attracted to. This was life-altering to me. She wasn't loving me in spite of the way I dressed and expressed my gender, she was loving me because of it. And something in me knew that if she could love this about me, the way had already been paved for me to accept and love it too.

Through these transformative exchanges, our energetic bond across the miles proved to be a dance of light and shadow mirroring the complexity of our souls. We were showing each other the way home, back to self, and to love. The synchronicities felt like the universe conspiring to align our paths. Navigating the unknown, we stepped into many uncharted territories together, guided by unseen forces orchestrating our journey. As the symphony of our connection played on, I realized that the magic in our mess wasn't about escaping challenges but about finding enchantment, growth, and self-acceptance within them. This relationship was increasing my capacity to love, which included the way I loved myself. I'd have to get back on the emotional roller coaster, I knew, but I would embrace each twist and turn, knowing that the magic of our connection could turn any mess into a masterpiece.

Chapter 19

Awakening

In high school, I had often thought about when and how I'd lose my virginity, believing it would mark the pinnacle of intimacy. I hoped it would finally fill the void of loneliness and lack of self-worth I had carried for so long.

But high school passed without any magical moments. I didn't attend prom, never had a boyfriend, and graduated a virgin. I felt like the loser character from those teen movies, the one who never gets to experience the rite of passage meant for the main character. My worries only intensified as I entered college. Would I be the only virgin there? Was something wrong with me?

College life began, and my friends started dating while I remained on the sidelines. No one approached me, and my self-doubt followed me. I craved a boyfriend more than anything; it seemed like the answer to my problems. Just when I thought it was happening for me with Steve, it fell apart in the most painful way possible. My encounter with him quickly went from flirting and butterflies to rape. I never saw it coming. Just like that, I was the victim I never thought I'd be. I sank so low and began to seek promiscuity, a game I played shamefully. I'd pursue guys who seemed out of my league, engage in meaningless encounters, and then disappear from their lives. It was a desperate attempt to convince myself that sex was meaningless and that what happened to me in the woods that night was no big deal. I needed to believe that.

Eventually, I secured a boyfriend, but it didn't bring the happiness I expected. He treated me poorly and cheated on me, reinforcing my belief that I wasn't lovable. I clung to him desperately, thinking it was better to have something than nothing. When he finally broke up with me, I felt like I was back where I started: empty-handed, broken, discarded. I hated this part of my story, so I locked it away, never telling a soul about the rape. I despised myself and indulged in reckless behavior, but it was all a facade—a way to hide the pain and self-hatred deep inside me.

Years passed, and I still craved that true, intimate connection I had dreamed about since high school. I carried that desire with me throughout many relationships, and just when I'd thought it wasn't meant to be, life took this unexpected turn. It took falling in love with a woman to experience all the firsts I had missed—including my first kiss with Kelly. It was a moment I knew would be more magical than I could even imagine. The anticipation filled me with nervousness, excitement, and wonder.

* * *

Kelly and I made plans to meet in Denver; she needed to come to Colorado for some other business anyway, and since it happened to be my birthday weekend, we decided we'd spend a few days together—our first several days, and nights, together as a couple.

As the weekend approached, I woke up early, feeling like a child on Christmas morning. I fantasized about what she would wear, how it would feel to hold her, and what her lips would taste like. It was a birthday celebration I would never forget, and it was just a few days away. I was equal parts nervous and giddy, filled with expectation and a heightened awareness of my inexperience. I realized that my previous relationships couldn't possibly have prepared me for what it was like to be intimate with my person, a true love, but I also knew nothing about how to be with a woman.

My anticipation reached its peak as I prepared for our date, which I had gone shopping for at one of the few clothing stores in Eagle County. Similar to the selection at REI, most of the clothing was sports and outdoorwear. For the first time, I allowed myself to venture into the men's section. I kept looking over my shoulder like I was going to be arrested by the gender police at any moment. I indulged in all the clothes I always wished I could have, trying on different garments and spending time with each one. I settled on a pair of jeans that rode low on my waist and a blue, ultra-soft Kuhl men's shirt that had a zipper on the sleeve.

That morning, I pulled out the new jeans and shirt and put them on with such pride. I showered, groomed, and primped, savoring each moment. No longer bound by societal expectations, I excitedly dressed in this outfit that felt authentic to me. I put on my new boxer underwear—magic—my favorite sports bra, a white T-shirt, and pulled the blue shirt with the zipper on the sleeve over top. I felt so amazing; I felt *sexy*! I'd had many first dates, but this was the first time I truly felt like myself.

Finally, I was in the car, en route to pick Kelly up from the airport. Nervousness coursed through my veins as I watched the clock, counting down the minutes. The two-hour car ride felt like two days, each minute painfully, slowly ticking down. I couldn't believe that I was about to kiss Kelly. I couldn't wait for her plane to arrive.

I got to the airport and parked in short-term parking. While I normally picked family up curbside at the airport, this felt special. I needed to meet her inside. I found a spot about twenty spaces from the door and nervously checked myself in the tiny rearview mirror before leaving and locking the car.

I quickly walked to the sliding door of the airport and breezed inside. The air was brisk in September, but I hadn't worn a jacket, because I didn't want to cover up my amazing new blue shirt. The warm heat of the airport was like a reassuring hug. I walked past baggage claim and found my way to the area where passengers would leave the secure area. Several people formed a circle around the escalator ascending from the shuttle that brought them from the terminals. Many had roses, signs, and balloons. I didn't, but I had a huge hug and a kiss waiting for my girl.

I was so nervous, I imagined the other people in the airport could feel heat radiating off of me. I noticed my mouth was beyond dry. I couldn't kiss Kelly with cottonmouth, so I speed-walked over to a coffee cart vendor and bought a water. I took a huge swig and put the bottle in my back pocket. Somehow, this felt cool to me.

I kept watching each head emerge as travelers came up the escalator: *not her, not her, not her. Where is she? Is she coming? Did she change her mind?* My stomach turned in knots. I saw someone ascend with a Nashville hat on. *This must be her flight*, I thought.

The moment I saw her, I felt a rush of emotions. She didn't see me at first and started walking past me. I rushed to catch up to her, touching her on the shoulder from behind. She spun around and our eyes met, with huge smiles and tears in our eyes. We hugged tightly, both trembling with nerves. Then, I kissed her. It was awkward and a little stiff, but I felt so proud of myself for doing it! It was as if all the misalignments of my past had been corrected, and I was finally okay.

We walked to the parking garage, hand in hand. We

wandered the garage looking for my car, laughing and kissing. Everything felt soft, kind, and full of okay-ness. I was smitten, acting like a teenager in love, and I didn't care. In my anticipation, I hadn't paid attention to where I parked, but it didn't matter. I was proud of the person I was becoming, and I cherished every moment with Kelly.

Eventually, we spotted the car, and I shook my head in disbelief, grinning at my love-induced absentmindedness. As we sat in the car, our lips met again, and this time, our tongues danced. It was electrifying, turning me on in a way I had never experienced before. Every cell in my body felt alive, and tears welled up in my eyes.

As our lips finally parted, and I gazed into Kelly's eyes, I felt an overwhelming sense of healing wash over me. It was as if the broken parts of my soul, the wounds from my college years, were being mended with each tender kiss and every loving touch. This was not just a first kiss; it was a profound revelation that everything I had once believed had been stolen from me was now being delivered in abundance. The magic I had yearned for, the profound connection I had sought, was all unfolding before me in ways more beautiful and perfect than I had ever dared to imagine. After years of despair and self-doubt, I was finally discovering the truest, most authentic version of myself, and it was a journey filled with wonder, love, and the promise of an extraordinary future.

Falling in love with Kelly made the world around me disappear, leaving only the two of us in a bubble of euphoria. Everything felt like a miracle, and even the simplest things became extraordinary. That first kiss with Kelly was a revelation. It was a moment that exceeded all my expectations, transforming the world into a place of boundless wonder.

As we sat in that car, time didn't exist—every second was an eternity of bliss that made my heart swelled with joy. The feeling was akin to the moment I received my first pair of perfectly fitting ski boots as a child. It was as if I had spent my life skiing on borrowed equipment, never realizing that something so much better was within reach. With Kelly, everything just clicked into place, like a perfect carve on freshly groomed slopes.

Kissing had always held a special place in my heart, as it felt more intimate to me than sex itself. Yet, with men, it had often felt lacking, like trying to replicate a cherished family recipe that never quite turned out the same. But kissing Kelly was different. Her touch was gentle, her lips soft, and her tongue pure magic, sending ripples of sensation throughout my body. It was a whole new level of connection and intimacy.

Kelly had surprised me with a reservation at a luxurious hotel, which a birthday gift almost too good to be real—it was a dream come true. As we drove there, I couldn't help but marvel at how surreal it all was. I felt so cherished and cared for. We pulled up at the valet and a hotel employee immediately greeted us.

"Checking in?" he asked.

I blushed and offered a sheepish, "Yes." When he asked for the last name, I stammered my own and then realized that for the first time ever, I hadn't been the one to make the reservation.

I felt like a kid with a fake ID trying to order their first drink. Did everyone know we were here to make out? To have sex for the first time?

Walking in, we headed for the front reception. The art in the lobby was incredible, and the fountain in the corner gave it a ritzy feel. This was a five-star hotel, for sure. Checking in at the desk, I couldn't shake the feeling that everyone around us somehow knew we were in love, about to experience something profound. I felt proud, almost brazen, as if wearing a badge that declared, "Lesbians in love."

The walk to the elevator felt endless, but with every passing moment, my desire for Kelly grew stronger. As the elevator doors closed to take us up to our floor, we reached for each other just as the doors opened again. We quickly pulled apart and looked out at a nondescript woman staring back at us, clutching a duffel bag in her hands. I could feel my face turning red as the woman gave us a quick smile, and Kelly and I held in our laughter as the doors opened and she got off at the next floor. When the doors closed again, we burst into laughter.

Upon entering our room, it was as if we had stepped into a penthouse suite. The elegant decor, a kitchenette with champagne glasses and a plate of fruit and chocolates, all felt like a fantasy. I felt like a celebrity, and it was absolutely amazing.

As I looked at Kelly, her body clothed in a perfect-fitting T-shirt, my longing for her intensified. I wanted to explore every inch of her, to see her naked, to taste her skin. And, for the first time in my life, I felt confident and sure of myself. A new aspect of my personality had awakened, one filled with swagger and desire, a part of me I had never known before.

Taking the lead, I boldly suggested we check out the bed, and it felt both exhilarating and surreal to be so forward. But it was different this time; it wasn't about taking or getting something. It was about sharing and connecting with Kelly on a profound level.

Our exploration of each other was a journey without a destination. It wasn't about reaching a climax; it was about the connection we shared, both physically and emotionally. Every touch, every kiss, was an expression of our love. I wanted to honor her, to make sure she was comfortable, to gain her consent every step of the way. It wasn't about rushing; it was about savoring every moment.

For the first time, I wasn't driven by a goal, but by a deepening sense of intimacy. This shared experience was about being present with each other, body and soul. Making love to Kelly was healing for both of us, a way of undoing the damage of past experiences.

As we bathed together in the tub, I felt completely comfortable in my own skin. Gone were my shame and self-judgment. With Kelly's love and acceptance, I was learning to love and accept myself. Our physical bodies were no longer the most important aspect of being naked together; it was about being emotionally, mentally, and spiritually vulnerable.

This was just the beginning of a profound journey of love and self-discovery, where the physical act of making love was just one facet of a much larger connection. It was a journey that would forever change my perspective on intimacy and the true meaning of love. As we lay together in that warm bath, bodies exposed, hearts wide open, and souls entwined, I knew with unwavering certainty that the risk was worth it. In that moment, life was richer, and love was boundless. More than just finding myself, I had found a profound, magical connection in the beautiful mess of it all.

Chapter 20

Witness

For most of my life, telling people that I had fallen in love had been a joyful, celebratory experience. Of course, there were always challenging conversations with my dad about the guys I was dating, but those seemed like trivial hurdles. "I met someone" was typically followed by the familiar script of enthusiastic curiosity. But as I contemplated sharing the news of my newfound love with others, nothing could have prepared me for the profound shift that awaited me.

Stephen, my longtime coach and confidant, seemed like a natural place to start—but even so, this was uncharted territory. Stephen had been my mentor of over 10 years. He spoke a spiritual language I could barely understand, but I knew there was so much he could teach me. He was so committed to self-growth, which resonated with me so deeply. I desperately wanted to learn from him, so I knew he'd be the perfect person to share this new growth journey with.

The idea of revealing my relationship with Kelly to the world left me with a complex cocktail of emotions, all excitement and trepidation stirred together in an intricate chemistry. It wasn't merely announcing that I had found love; it was a greater revelation that came with an added layer of vulnerability. I also needed to disclose that my new love defied societal norms—it was a love for someone of the same sex.

The excitement was palpable, but the nervous anticipation of unveiling a deeply personal aspect of my identity was entwined in it. My mind swirled in a tempest of questions and uncertainty: *Have I always been gay? Is my sexuality fluid, or has it undergone a transformation? Am I gay, bisexual, lesbian, pansexual, or something else entirely?* I was navigating the uncharted waters inside without a map, a compass, or even the stars to guide me.

The realization that I loved a woman so profoundly yet had never recognized this aspect of myself was both exhilarating and bewildering. *How did I not know? Is this a recent change, or had it been an undiscovered truth begging to be seen throughout my entire life?* Despite years of inner exploration, the flood of questions threatened to overwhelm me.

As I grappled with it all, I felt consumed by a desperate desire for guidance and understanding. I craved a community that could comprehend the seismic shift in my world, offering insights and support as I navigated through it. Books, stories, and conversations became my compass, a way to set a course through the storm of my evolving identity.

On the day I finally told someone about Kelly, the setting mirrored the tumult within. Originally, I had planned to spend two days in Denver at suicide intervention training. The training was canceled last minute, but the hotel stay was nonrefundable, and now, a decision loomed. Should I spend two days at home confronting solitude and allowing my anxiety about needing to tell someone to take root, or should I retreat from the discomfort and drive to Denver anyway?

I thought I could use the hotel stay as a little retreat for myself, a time for some self-care, and so, the choice was made. Armed with books, a journal, and the weight of my newfound truth, I left the house and embarked on a drive, the world still cloaked in the quietude of dawn. The familiar ritual of morning tea at a coffee shop, a momentary distraction from the impending revelation, provided a semblance of routine.

Amid the quiet comfort of my car, Kelly's text arrived, breaking the silence:

Good morning!

Its simplicity still carried a weight that filled me with profound joy. A subsequent surprise—a Spotify playlist crafted for my drive—appeared on the screen like an unexpected gift, evoking emotions I thought were reserved for teenage rites of passage.

The first song that played was our song, "You and Me on the

Rock." Its lyrics, once distant, now resonated as if written for us. Each subsequent song felt like a puzzle piece fitting into the mosaic of our love story. It was a revelation that transcended mere acknowledgment; it was a recognition of a love that had always been present, waiting to be unveiled. As I neared the hotel, Kelly called, and her familiar filled me with warmth. Once again, our conversation flowed effortlessly, and I was savoring her every word.

The hotel, though far from luxurious, became our cocoon, a space to rest before confronting the reality that would soon unfold. The decision to confide in Stephen still loomed before me like a precipice. Staring at his name on my phone, the gravity of what I was about to do gripped me. As if I were about to step onstage, my entire body was hesitating, clenched from the nerves. I let my finger hover over his number before finally pressing it, the decision now made.

The call initiated, and I barely had time to register I'd pressed my finger to the screen when I heard Stephen's familiar, comforting voice on the other end—a voice that had been a sanctuary through countless other moments of vulnerability. The knot of emotions wound within me began to unravel themselves, turning into tears and confessions.

"I'm in love with one of my best friends," I began tearfully. "And she's a woman."

The words, once confined within me, were now free. A confession of love—and an initiation of a journey of self-discovery, of showing the world, one person at a time, who I truly was.

The admission hung in the air. The response on the other end, gentle and affirming, provided a lifeline.

"I'm here," Stephen said. It was a simple declaration, but it resonated with unconditional love and acceptance. As tears streamed down my face, I felt both vulnerable and relieved. This was the first step, the opening of a chapter that had long been concealed. That specter of rejection that had always loomed so large was gradually dissipating in the warmth of Stephen's support.

"Tell me more," he urged—a familiar refrain that was now inviting me to delve into the complexities of my newfound love.

For the next 20 minutes, I poured out my heart to Stephen, unveiling the story of my connection with Kelly. I navigated my unfamiliar emotional terrain, grappling with the intricacies of a love that transcended conventional boundaries. Articulating all my feelings was cathartic and therapeutic; they had remained dormant for far too long. Stephen, such an adept confidant and guide, offered insights that became guiding lights in the labyrinth of my emotions.

"This is a gift," he reminded me, another refrain of his that echoed through the uncertainty. The acknowledgment that I had discovered true love, regardless of its unconventional nature, became a beacon of hope amid the tumult.

Along with these revelations of the beauty of love, a paradox clarified: my joy of newfound connection was juxtaposed with my fear of societal judgment and personal upheaval. The love that felt like a lifeline also posed a challenge to the foundations of my identity—with family, friends, and career all hanging in precarious balance.

This aspect of coming out, I realized, was a nuanced dance of revelation and risk. The fear of judgment would lurk with each disclosure, an ever-present shadow in the journey of unveiling my authentic self. The narratives of acceptance and rejection played out like delicate chemical interactions, and I became acutely aware of the fragility of relationships.

The days that followed were a mosaic of emotions. Each conversation with friends became a litmus test for our connection, a measure of the strength of our bonds. Some embraced my revelation with immediate warmth and support, while others met it with awkward silences or redirection. But through it all, Kelly remained a steadfast companion, a source of love that could weather the storms of uncertainty. Together, we faced the challenges that came with embracing an unconventional love.

Though those conversations were laden with painful moments, they also brought unexpected allies and newfound strength. Not every connection survived the authenticity test, and some of my friendships crumbled under the weight of judgment. It had all revealed the true colors of those I considered close, and the losses were palpable. Still, it all cleared space for new, authentic connections to take root.

As I navigated this labyrinth of emotions, shed layers of

false identity, a profound sense of liberation emerged. Coming out, as messy as it was, became a powerful act of self-love. I was cleaning out my closet, letting go of items that had never served me and embracing those that held true value.

The pain of rejection was real, but it was eclipsed by the overwhelming support of those who chose to stand beside me. Coming out was transformative, demanding courage, resilience, and an unwavering commitment to self-discovery.

Reflecting on that period of my life, I recognize the beauty in the chaos. Coming out was not just a revelation of sexual orientation; it was an affirmation of love in all its forms. The closet, once a symbol of secrecy, was transformed into a metaphor for rebirth and self-acceptance. I stepped out of that closet not only as a declaration of love for Kelly, but as a proclamation of love for myself. The arduous journey was worth every painful step, as it led to a newfound strength and a profound connection with those who embraced me wholeheartedly.

Coming out was not just an ending; it was a beginning—a beginning of a life lived authentically, unburdened by societal expectations. By embracing my identity, I discovered the magic of self-love, a force that transcends boundaries and transforms individuals and the world around them.

As I extended an invitation to self-discovery, resilience, and the pursuit of love in all its forms, I began to recognize the darkness of the closet as a prelude to the brilliance of authenticity. Stepping into the light and embracing the truth was a way to show the world the beauty of my unfiltered, unapologetic self. As ever, love remained the guiding force that led us out of the shadows and into the brilliance of our truest selves.

Chapter 21

The Last to Know

After dialing Stephen, one of my first calls was to Bishop Karen Oliveto of the Mountain Sky Conference of the United Methodist Church.

Karen Oliveto is not just any bishop—she's the first openly lesbian bishop in the United Methodist Church. I figured reaching out to her was like stepping into slightly safer territory than telling my own congregation, so she seemed like a logical next step. I dialed her after thinking back to our first encounter, during my inaugural day at seminary at Iliff School of Theology. She was teaching a class called Prophetic Leadership. As our first course wrapped up, I decided to muster the courage to talk to her amid the shuffling of bags, jackets, and coffee cups.

Bishop Oliveto, warm and approachable though she was, still carried an air of intimidation. I didn't want to kick off our potential friendship by saying something weird or, God forbid, stupid. Fumbling with my coat while juggling a protein shake, a water bottle, and a cup of tea, I psyched myself up, took a deep breath, and headed straight for her, bumping into other students as they exited the room. As I approached, I gave her my best smile, and she responded with a big hug, immediately using my name. Relief washed over me. *Phew, she knows who I am. This won't be so bad*, I thought.

"Thanks for such a fantastic start to seminary!" I said truthfully, acknowledging the impact I could already tell her course would have on me. Then, I decided to go for a classic move. "Can I get a picture with you?"

Bishop Oliveto welcomed my request with enthusiasm. The photo turned out great, except for the minor detail that I had forgotten to take off my coat first. *Rookie move*, I thought as I started gathering up all my cups to make my exit. Before I could even turn to the door, she dropped a bombshell.

"Molly, there are many support groups and resources for gay clergy in this area," she said. *Wait, what?* I thought. *Why did she say that?* Then it hit me: *The bishop thinks I'm gay. Great.* In that moment, I felt how strange it was to feel completely separate from the person I believed myself to be. After my conversation with Stephen, our interaction resurfaced from the depths of my memories, and I found myself dialing her office to leave a message. I needed to tell her, and I yearned to understand how she had known years ago what I was only now beginning to understand about myself.

Days later, as I was pulling into the post office parking lot, Bishop Oliveto's name popped up on my phone screen. I parked facing the bustling post office, bracing myself for the conversation. The sun beamed through the window, and I could feel the car heating up, mirroring the warmth rising in my insides. I took a deep breath and answered the call with my go-to nervous greeting: "Hi there."

"Hello, Molly," Bishop Oliveto, her voice ever comforting, began. "You called a few days ago. What's going on?"

"I'm in love with my friend, who is a woman," I blurted. There it was, out of my mouth and into the world. I was officially out to the bishop.

"Molly, I've been waiting for this call," she said, and I could practically feel her smile on the other end. *Had she really known back in seminary? What did she see or know that I didn't?* Relieved, yet perplexed, I found comfort in her lack of shock.

"Really? Not surprised at all?" I asked.

"The woman is the last to know," she said meaningfully. *Apparently so.* It felt incredibly unsettling, realizing I might be the last to know. *What was it about me that I couldn't see? How could she have known this before I did?* It's like I'd been walking around with a sign on my back my whole life, visible to everyone but me. And that bugged me. I wanted to know what I'd missed. *Was it the way I dress? Walk? Talk? Look?* My questions hung in the air like a joke with a misunderstood punchline. Before I could ask them, I started to ramble.

"I must have a teenager's brain," I said. "God, for weeks, I've been distracted, thinking about Kelly *all the time*. I feel like my hormones have hit me like a ton of bricks. I'm even daydreaming about kissing her! I *never* felt this way when I was actually a teen. It's like I was somehow put on a thirty-year delay. My productivity is in the gutter, and I'm consuming sugar like it's my job. I'm stressing about losing my superpower—my work ethic, my grit. Am I going to turn into a love-crazed flake? How am I ever going to get anything done?"

"Molly," the Bishop said with quiet confidence, "this kind of love doesn't come around that often. This is a gift. Relax and enjoy it!"

Right! I kept forgetting that for decades—for every birthday candle blown out, wishbone snapped, and coin tossed in a fountain—my prayer had been the same: "God, please give me true love." Now, here it was, and I was consumed with worry. This was a gift. I needed to unwrap it, not fret about it.

A few days later, back at home and armed with newfound courage, I decided to tell my dad. He was the one I was most worried about. I vividly remembered his judgmental statements about homosexuality when I was young. He once banned my little brother from the house for having an earring, deeming it "queer," so the fear coursing through me as I dialed his number made total sense.

"I've got some news to share, and it's hard," I said after brief pleasantries.

"Well, just spit it out," he replied, understandably impatient in the silence that followed. *Easier said than done,* I thought.

"I'm in love with my friend, and she's a woman," I announced. The pause that followed seemed endless. I sat at my desk, kicking my shoes off in a nervous panic. As the silence stretched, I curled and uncurled my toes on the carpet.

"Well, Molly... I'm not surprised," he said. *What?* The silence between us extended. "Probably not what you were expecting, huh?"

"No, not at all," I confessed. "I thought you were going to have all kinds of problems with this."

"Yeah, I can see why you'd think that," he said simply. "You've never had good relationships with men, and you've struggled so much. If this is what makes you happy, then I'm thrilled for you. I just want you to have someone to do life with. I've worried about that for you. So, this is kind of a relief for me, actually."

Completely floored and at a loss for words, I stared at my feet, rubbing them on the carpet. Then, Dad started asking about Kelly and how we met, and I felt giddy. This was the fun part, sharing the crazy love story. I jumped straight into the tale excitedly, not realizing the privilege of being able to start with the love story rather than needing to tiptoe around the whole "I'm in love with a woman" part.

As we talked, my dad shared how he had seen signs and this revelation made sense to him. He remembered how I never seemed interested in boys and struggled in past relationships. I was flabbergasted. How had he seen all this when I couldn't? I had buried this part of myself so deeply that even when someone else pointed it out, I struggled to comprehend it.

As the conversation continued, I felt a mix of emotions. On one hand, there was relief that my dad was accepting and supportive. On the other hand, there was a profound sense of discomfort. How had I missed all these signs? How did everyone else see it before I did? It felt like I'd walking around with a neon sign on my forehead, and I had been the last to know what it said.

Coming out, for me, wasn't just about revealing my identity to others; it was also about discovering and accepting it for myself. The journey was a complex mix of relief, confusion, gratitude, and, at times, frustration. The realization that others knew me in ways I didn't know myself was a hard pill to swallow.

Six months later, during a trip to Nashville to visit Kelly, we went to see comedian Fortune Feimster at the Ryman, who shared her own coming out experience. Weeks earlier, on a weekend getaway, we had binged a ton of comedy shows, Feimster's among them. Listening to her was like hearing a long-lost sister talk about your childhood. I couldn't get enough of her humor, so naturally, we jumped at the chance to see her live.

Feimster's brothers had responded to her coming out with a nonchalant "duh." As I laughed in deep, belly-shaking bursts, I related so much to her timing and expressions. It's like she was saying from the stage what I had been thinking and experiencing for months. That unique feeling of recognition that I wasn't alone was one of the greatest sensations on the planet.

"Cool, cool," she continued. "Well, thanks for telling me

that. You didn't want to tell me that when I was walking down the aisle in a white wedding gown?"

Yes! Same! Why hadn't someone clued me in on this before my first marriage? Or even my second one! That would have saved me so much heartache, angst, and money! But the next line hit me right in the core.

Feimster asked how her brothers had known this the whole time. She started to say her brothers' response was to tell a story of a time when she had gotten hit with a soccer ball when she was younger. I had two brothers growing up, so that was already relatable, but I was hanging on her every word after having been hit with a soccer ball so many times when I was about the same age. I couldn't wait for the punch line.

I was on pins and needles to hear what this "gay thing" was that she had done that she hadn't been able to see. Apparently, as her brothers told her, Feimster had crumpled over when the ball hit her and said, "Ow, my dick!"

I laughed even harder. She was sharing my story, my words, my experiences.

"Clearly, I was very confused," she continued—*Yes! Me too!*Looking at things in the rearview mirror of my mind, there had been so many more dick punches. I had tried to dress like a boy my whole life. Several of my childhood friends had come out not long after high school, and it hadn't occurred to me until that moment that many of my best friends were gay. I had played college women's rugby for *four years*. How had I missed that one? I had a black lab and drove a Subaru. The signs were there, the lights just hadn't been turned on. Clearly, *I* was very confused.

In the days and weeks that followed the comedy show, I reflected on the layers of my identity I had hidden—not only from others, but from myself. I questioned why it had taken so long for me to acknowledge my own truth. *Why did I suppress all these feelings and all these aspects of my identity for so many years?* I wondered. This question lingered in my mind like an echo in an empty room.

* * *

The journey of self-discovery is often filled with twists and turns, and sometimes it takes the reflections of others to illuminate the hidden corners of our own identities. While the revelations were unsettling, they also opened doors to self-acceptance and authenticity. As I navigated this new chapter of my life, I began to appreciate the complexities of human identity. It wasn't just about being gay; it was about embracing the full spectrum of who I am. The process of self-discovery didn't end with coming out; it marked the beginning of a deeper exploration into the intricacies of my own being.

The realization that others had insights into my identity before I did taught me the importance of humility. It reminded me that growth and self-awareness are ongoing processes. None of us have all the answers about ourselves, and that's okay. Life is a journey of continuous learning, and sometimes, others can offer valuable perspectives that we might have overlooked.

Self-discovery is a personal and, at times, challenging journey. I didn't have all the answers, and I still don't. I'm learning
that it's okay to embrace the uncertainties that come with
understanding oneself. The journey of coming out is not just
about revealing our truths to the world; it's about uncovering
and accepting those truths within ourselves and gaining a
deeper understanding of the beautiful complexities that make
each of us uniquely human.

Chapter 22

The Price Is High

S elf-discovery and truly embracing my newfound self didn't come without risk. To embrace Kelly meant laying it all on the line—family, friends, identity, career, faith, home, community—all of it. I had to let go of everything I knew about myself, and open up to a new chapter in my life. Was this the universal queer experience? I had already taken leaps with Stephen and Dad. Next was my brother.

Telling Willy was pretty uneventful. Feimster, the comedian, had said her brothers responded to her coming out with a "Duh!" Willy reacted very similarly—he was super supportive and wasn't that surprised. He told me he and my parents had been worried about my relationship struggles over the years. They had worried for so long about me being alone, and for the first time, it seemed to them like I had found my person. They were all delighted.

After I talked to Dad, he kept my secret for a week before I mustered the courage to tell Mom. I realized as we were talking that my hesitation really stemmed from the clothes issue. I felt I was always letting my mom down with my style. I was never into fashion or cute girl clothes, and I knew it had weighed on her. My mom went to school for fashion; meanwhile, her daughter loved soccer clothes. I could still remember her looking longingly at cute girl or teen clothes and sighing, knowing I'd never even try them on.

My clothing choices and sexuality were inexorably linked in my mind, and I worried my mom would be disappointed. I also felt some anger at her for living in an environment where I'd felt so suppressed as a kid. I think I was afraid to tell her for fear that it would be like the clothes again—I'd have to compromise or not get what I wanted, and I didn't want to ruin how amazing I felt. But when the time came, she seemed to take it pretty well.

When clothes came up, she simply said, "Oh, Molly, I gave that up years ago." Funny, I hadn't. I was still policing myself and feeling like she was looking over my shoulder. I felt so much judgment and pressure, but I now realize that most of it wasn't actually coming from her.

Once I had come out unscathed to my closest circle—Dad, Mom, my brother, and Stephen—I felt a little relief, but I knew the journey was far from over. There was still a big hurdle that remained: telling the church. My sexuality now played a central role in everything, in stark contrast to all my prior life experience. It felt absurd and stressful, akin to confessing a secret drug habit that could jeopardize my work. Decades of building my professional reputation seemed overshadowed by this new piece of information.

The church was a complex entity comprised of various disconnected parts—the local leadership, a district superintendent, a bishop, the cabinet, and the Board of Ordained Ministry. Telling the church meant informing each of these entities separately, and each was a separate snag in the tapestry I was weaving with Kelly.

The United Methodist Church was grappling with a schism over gay clergy, so my timing couldn't have made my position more precarious. The debate, simmering for decades, had reached a boiling point, and the appointment of an openly gay bishop in 2016 intensified the tension. As I navigated my first same-sex relationship while serving as a pastor, the global church was on the brink of a decisive vote on the issue.

Where to start? Bishop Oliveto had offered some support, and the Mountain Sky Conference, with Bishop Oliveto at the helm, seemed a relatively affirming conference. However, I knew that certain churches within my conference might not be accepting. Questions flooded my mind: *Will I be kicked out? How will my congregation react? What does this mean for my future as a pastor and my upcoming ordination? Did I want to be a gay pastor in the UMC?*

The clear path I once saw was now muddled, and all the internal conflict I felt during the ordination process resurfaced. The uncertainty was overwhelming—my career, faith commu nity, livelihood, and housing all hung in the balance. How could I reconcile my deep calling to serve the church with a relationship the church deemed sinful?

Once I had mentally decided to tell the church, everything else that had to follow felt like it was going in fast forward. My urgency to share my truth was consumed me, and I couldn't seem to convey it fast enough. It mirrored my approach to facing fear: You had to jump in without overthinking it. It made me feel like I was a kid again, standing on the edge of a rock at Lake Powell. The longer I hesitated, the harder it became. I wanted to leap and see where I landed.

After my call with Bishop Oliveto, I decided to start at the top with the district superintendent. In the front seat of the small, familiar space of my blue Toyota 4Runner, I dialed the district superintendent, trying to find solace in the faint hint of Otis's scent. Nervous energy circled in my belly. As the inside of the car got warmer, I turned it off to eliminate the extra noise. It was a strange setting for another pivotal coming-out call.

As the phone rang, I felt the heat of the phone on my cheek. I tried to play out the conversation in my mind, to anticipate the superintendent's reaction. Part of me had wished for voicemail, but when she answered, I knew it was time to jump. I had been so desperate to take the plunge for far too long. Fear enveloped me—would she approve, be disappointed, or alter my appointment? I felt like I was putting all my power and reputation in her hands. This vulnerability, however, was also a moment of empowerment. I wasn't seeking approval; I was declaring my truth.

Ultimately, the district superintendent's response was the affirmation I needed to hear. It was good news—she celebrated the opportunity to experience such love, emphasizing its rarity. Even as I rejoiced internally over her acceptance, I was frustrated by the power dynamics. My dependence on her affirmation irked me. *Why did I even need to make this call?* I thought. *Why was I so afraid?*

Looking back, I see that each coming out experience was more about breaking my own chains than fearing that others would put chains on me. I was afraid not just of the potential loss of relationships, but of liberating myself from the need for approval and validation. Unbeknownst to me, my connections were threaded with the necessity for agreement and approval, especially regarding my sexuality. Coming out was a reckoning with all the compromises I had made, all the contorting I'd done to fit others' expectations.

My liberation depended on relinquishing my need for approval. Each disclosure was a risk, a step away from conforming to others' expectations and toward authentic self-expression and loyalty to my own soul. It was a painful journey, like a chiropractic adjustment, but the rewards would be immeasurable.

As I took one step after another to align my life with my newfound authenticity, I felt trapped between a rock and a hard place. A lifetime of trying not to disappoint others had become second nature, but being with Kelly meant facing the inevitable: I would disappoint some people.

My old way of being no longer served me, and I had to

confront it head-on. I couldn't step into the next phase of my life with the same patterns. Putting my needs before the church was the most challenging thing I'd ever done, but deep down, I knew it was the right choice.

My heart raced with excitement and trepidation. I had known for a while that moving to Nashville was certain, and the opportunity to be with the love of my life was an adventure filled with the unknown. Leaving behind everything I had known for 46 years—my community, friends, and family—added to the mix of emotions. But there was something more I had to leave behind: the congregation.

After I had come out to everyone, there was still one more thing to do that probably one of the most painful, and that was to leave. It didn't seem workable or fair to have Kelly, Lucy, and Rick move, and the dynamics of our friend group in Eagle were already strained. I knew if we wanted to be together, I would have to go to Nashville. I had to, but I also wanted to.

Even before anything happened with Kelly, I had felt a nudge about Nashville. I even remembered telling her once, long before our airport conversation, that I had thought about moving there. I had no idea why, but the Spirit was tugging me in that direction even then.

Leaving my church appointment wasn't a decision I took lightly. I cherished my community and believed there was more

I could contribute. Things were going well, and leaving that behind felt incredibly challenging. Still, I knew it was what I needed to do. I agonized over how to break the news to the church leadership, fearing their disappointment. My plan was to leave UMC of Eagle Valley, move to Nashville, and take a year-long leave of absence from preaching to heal, reflect, and find my footing after this life-altering realization about myself.

The leave of absence was approved by the conference, but sharing my decision with the local congregation was heart-wrenching. They wanted me to stay, which only made leaving harder. It seemed to hurt them that the pain seemed one-sided—but it wasn't. I felt it too, but as I always had, I tried to maintain emotional distance.

Sticking to my decision tore me apart and was one of the toughest choices I'd ever made, but I knew it was right. I needed time away from the leadership role. I had lost two dear friends to cancer during Covid, and my heart was aching with grief on top of everything else. Leading a congregation through the pandemic left me emotionally drained, and I was running on empty. My world had just been turned upside down, and I needed time to breathe and take care of my mind, body, and spirit. This was the choice that would honor myself and the congregation the most. However, not everyone saw it the same way.

Some saw it as quitting, and I received feedback suggesting I should tough it out. It was the the old "suck it up and be tough" mindset from my childhood all over again. I had often pushed through trauma, depression, fatigue, burnout, and even a suicidal crisis for the sake of others. Taking time off was unfamiliar territory, but the most significant challenge was facing others' disappointment without trying to fix it. Because I wanted to manage their emotions, I overcompensated by offering to serve the church remotely. It was my way of holding on while taking the leap, but it didn't work. They set a hard boundary and declined my offer.

Though I desperately wanted to fix everything, I knew I couldn't. People were upset and disappointed, and their pain was profound. Their words stung, but I stood firm in my decision, navigating through the difficult conversations and emotional blows. Then came the knockout punch.

Although my leave of absence had been approved by the conference, the Board of Ordained Ministry had different plans. I had thought that with a mental health leave of absence, everything church-related would be on hold for a year, but that wasn't the case in my ordination process. I would still need to meet with the board as scheduled during my leave of absence or face discontinuation.

I didn't mind still needing to have the interview; in fact, I welcomed it. I had questions about my call to ministry and was eager to discuss them with the board. I worked out the details to reschedule the meeting as a video call rather than an in-person interview, but I had missed a crucial detail. I assumed my request for a virtual meeting, which was approved, would mean a change in the time and date. I waited for a new time, but it never arrived.

As the original interview time drew near, I reached out to several board members for clarification, but I heard nothing until it was too late. I missed the email with the Zoom invite, and my interview date passed without me. My stomach sank, and I called my lead person on the board, explaining the misunderstanding and my availability. Later that day, I received a voicemail from the head of my reading team, delivering the news: I had missed my interview, and the board had voted to discontinue me.

I couldn't believe it. Seven years of dedication and hard work wiped out because of one missed Zoom call? The decision felt harsh, and I was left in shock. I waited for a follow-up call from the church—a word of explanation, guidance, or simply some pastoral care. But the calls never came. I had been fired, and I had lost everything—my home, salary, career, faith community, and colleagues. In a two-minute voicemail, my entire world crumbled. A door had slammed shut on me, leaving me feeling rejected, abandoned, and discarded. It was a shocking and devastating turn of events that left me bewildered and hurt.

The aftermath of my sudden and shocking expulsion from the church left me reeling. I was leaving a chapter of my life in a way I had never anticipated, and the pain of it was both profound and deeply disorienting. I questioned the fairness, kindness, and compassion of the faith community that had meant so much to me, but as the days turned into weeks, the shock began to subside. I realized that sometimes, the most painful door slams can lead to other unexpected openings.

In the midst of my grief and confusion, I began to glimpse the possibility of redefining my path, exploring my spirituality in different ways, and continuing my journey of self-discovery. It was a daunting prospect, but it held the promise of transformation and growth. The closed door had left me wounded, but it had also set me on a healing path toward a deeper understanding of myself.

As I navigated the uncertainty of what lay ahead, I clung to the belief that even in the darkest moments, there was potential for light to break through. The shock and grief of getting kicked out of the church reshaped my life in ways I could never have foreseen. Though the pain was real, I was determined to emerge stronger, more authentic, and with a renewed sense of purpose.

Despite my determination, in the aftermath of my expulsion from the church, I still found myself plunged into a pit of darkness, grappling with a heavy cloud of self-doubt and despair. The abrupt end to my career in ministry left me questioning everything I had ever known about myself. Maybe the church was right: perhaps I wasn't cut out for this path. The gnawing doubt grew louder, echoing the whispers of uncertainty that had plagued me for years. *Had I ever truly been meant for ministry?* I wondered. *Had it all been a mistake?*

I stood at a crossroads, facing challenges I had never encountered before. For the first time in my life, I was without a clear path forward, and the future seemed like an abyss of uncertainty. Worries about financial stability, career prospects, and the shape of my life going forward gnawed at me relentlessly. The weight of my failure bore down upon me, and I couldn't help but ask myself: *What have I done to deserve this?* The rejection felt like a dagger through my heart.

I dwelled on all the dreams I'd harbored for so long, dreams that were now shattered—dreams of being a United Methodist Church pastor, of leading a congregation, and making a meaningful impact within the church community. It was a time of mourning for all those lost dreams and for the future I had once envisioned.

One gloomy day, I decided to go for a run. My body moved mechanically, mirroring my low spirits. With each step, I felt the weight of rejection pressing down on me, a constant reminder of my perceived failure. As I jogged along, I contemplated the doors that had slammed shut in my face. The door to a UMC pastorship was firmly closed, but I wondered if it had ever been the right path for me at all.

In that moment, something shifted. I started to consider the closed door from a different perspective. What if this rejection, this loss, was clearing the path for something new, something more aligned with my authentic self? With this door firmly shut behind me, it was time to dream anew.

The dreams I had suppressed for years began to resurface. Writing, speaking, serving—these aspirations that had always lingered on the periphery of my consciousness now took center stage. What if the closed door was actually an invitation to embrace opportunities I had never dared to pursue? Could this setback be the catalyst for something extraordinary?

* * *

The pain of a closed door can be excruciating, and the sting of rejection can linger for a long time. But I've come to realize that behind every closed door lies a new beginning, a new opportunity for a fresh start. It's as if the universe is preparing us for something greater, something more aligned with our true purpose.

As I moved along on that solitary run, I began to embrace the uncertainty ahead. The closed door no longer felt like a barrier but a stepping stone on the path to a new adventure. What was God preparing me for? What was next? I was now headed into uncharted territory. I began to shift from labeling my expulsion from the church as my greatest failure to one of self-discovery and transformation, a prologue to an extraordinary beginning.

This journey would lead me to unexpected places and a deeper connection with my own spirituality. I had been pushed out into the unknown, but I was ready to embrace the adventure and discover the magic that could arise from the mess.

With Kelly on my mind and music playing in my ears as I ran, I listened to "Passionate Kisses" by Mary Chapin Carpenter was on repeat. I kept expecting the app to transition to the next song on the playlist, but it never happened, as if the universe wanted me to absorb every word. The lyrics were being etched into my soul with every stride:

Shouldn't I have this?

Is it too much to demand?
I shout it out to the night
Give me what I deserve, 'cause it's my right.

With each step, I felt a growing desire to shout, to scream from the mountaintops. *Damn right, it's my right! Shouldn't I have all of this? A true love, a big life, abundance, everything I've ever dreamed of?*

Until that moment, my answer had been a resounding "no." I had been conditioned to believe that I should be humble, that wanting more than what I had was somehow unspiritual. I had come to equate living simply with being virtuous and that desiring abundance was wrong, likely influenced by the notion of taking a vow of poverty.

This inner conflict gnawed at me. I couldn't help but ponder the life of Jesus, who lived simply and without excess. Was this the path I should be on? Was I greedy for wanting more, for desiring nice things? For too long, I had been imprisoned by the belief that I couldn't have nice things, and the more I clung to this idea, the more it shaped my reality.

Yet, as I ran that morning, a fire started to burn inside me. It was a fierce desire for more, a yearning for a big life, for going all-in. I had been playing small for far too long, diminishing myself and my dreams. A question that had been buried deep within me for years now surfaced: *What is the source of this burning dream? What would it take to go for it?*

But even as this newfound ambition began to take root, I felt the need to justify it: *Do I have to do good in the world to deserve a big life? Do I have to impact countless lives and change the world before it's okay to want more?* I thought about Oprah and her immense wealth. She was unapologetic, and I admired for her contributions. *Maybe if I could do good,* I thought, *I, too, could feel good about wanting abundance. But why am I placing this condition upon myself—the need to earn it, to prove myself worthy? What about simply wanting amazing things because they sound like so much fun?*

What kept reverberating within me was the idea of living one wild and crazy life. We only got this one shot, and I was done playing it safe. I wanted to take risks, to push the boundaries of what was possible, and to embrace every moment, regardless of the outcome. It was an embarrassing confession to make to myself, to utter these desires aloud, but I wanted to go for it. I wanted to live out loud and lead a big life, and I wanted *messy.* I wanted it all.

But even as these dreams ignited within me, I sensed hesitation. I had been holding back, playing it safe for so long that I still felt the pull to restrain myself. I asked myself why: *Why did I always play small?* With every jolt of my sneakers on the sidewalk, the answer became clearer and clearer: *I needed to belong. I wanted to fit in, to be liked, to avoid ridicule and judgment. I was more concerned with what others thought of me than with what I truly desired. I feared that pursuing big dreams would invite mockery and criticism, that I would be labeled a fool, unworthy of my aspirations.*

Coming out to my friends, family, church, and community was both a profound challenge and a tremendous gift. It taught me not to shrink in the presence of others, to face rejection and judgment head-on, to stop sacrificing myself on the altar of wanting to belong. I had chosen to be seen, to reveal my authentic self, and to say, "This is me, take me or leave me."

It was a new choice, and it was liberating. It gave me the courage to reach for more.

Chapter 23

A Little in the Middle

I asked myself a lot during those days: *Is balance the lesson life has in store for me?* After all, my rising sign is Libra, represented by the scales, an enduring symbol of balance. It seemed that no matter where my journey took me, I was consistently led back to this pivotal idea.

Throughout my life, I had been a force of unwavering determination, pushing boundaries and concealing inner turmoil behind a determined smile. This unrelenting drive for success spilled over into various aspects of my life—exercise, food, school, work—whatever held significance at the time. My motto was simple: "No pain, no gain."

This approach yielded results, but it exacted a steep price on my relationship with myself and on my body. My body ceased to trust my ability to heed its signals, to halt when it needed rest, or to provide a safe haven. I recklessly ignored its pleas, pushing it far beyond its limits. School, diet, exercise, and work became tools in my relentless pursuit, and I mercilessly berated myself for feeling tired (mistaken for laziness), slow (viewed as inadequacy), or uncertain (interpreted as stupidity). I had become my own drill sergeant, relentlessly pushing myself beyond physical and emotional thresholds. I believed that my ability to exert effort was my superpower. Yet, in the process, I fractured my connection with myself. I had disregarded my body for so long that it had fallen silent. I had pushed it to the brink one too many times.

Over the years, I had embarked on the painstaking journey of rebuilding that connection, slowing down, and actively listening. I had inquired about my body's needs and wants and patiently awaited its responses, which always arrived. Then came the arduous work of rebuilding trust, ensuring that when my body whispered fatigue, I genuinely rested; when it signaled hunger, I nourished it. Strangely, this proved challenging. I grappled with suppressing the urge to prove my worth and succumbing to the need for genuine self-care and self-love toward my body, which had endured so much.

When everything happened with Kelly, my appetite vanished. Lovesickness replaced my hunger, and I couldn't bear the thought of food. I'd make feeble attempts to consume something, believing it was an act of self-care, but every bite tasted like dirt. My appetite had been replaced by longing, and my body yearned for something different. I ate sparingly. My favorite coffee shop's egg salad sandwich and chips became a meal split between lunch and dinner, and I often left the chips untouched. I embraced this shift and attentively listened to my body's cues. Rapidly, I shed ten pounds, reaching a number I hadn't seen in years—128. It felt like an achievement, a sign that more work lay ahead. My body was rapidly letting go of weight, and I interpreted it as a positive sign. But what did "healthy" genuinely mean? I lacked a clear answer.

Initially, when I lost my appetite, an insatiable craving for sugar took its place. It was as if I had regressed to being ten years old, bingeing on candy at the corner store. Growing up with Ben, whose diabetes was always a concern, meant we had no sugar in the house—none at all. My occasional indulgences involved sneaking Luden's cherry cough drops and chewable vitamin C. When I had sleepovers at friends' houses, it meant going on candy sprees at the local gas station. I'd fill bags with Mambas, Skittles, Nerds, Jolly Ranchers, Smarties, and bubble gum, reveling in the array of choices. Suddenly, I was revisiting those days, purchasing four or five bags or boxes of candy every time I went to the store.

I hadn't consumed sugar like this since childhood. Throughout my thirties, I abstained from candy, only occasionally indulging in ice cream or dessert. Soda and candy were off-limits, barely crossing my mind. Yet now, it felt as if I were preparing for Halloween each time I ventured to the store. I'd sit in bed, queue up *Grey's Anatomy*, and consume Hi-Chews by the bag, never feeling satisfied. It was confounding.

Gradually, this pattern extended to other foods. I visited McDonald's for breakfast, something I hadn't done in over a decade. Ice cream became a staple, and my grocery cart transformed from a display of fruits, vegetables, and protein to a collection of candy, chips, and ice cream. I allowed myself to indulge, removing all restrictions. My weight skyrocketed to 145—the highest weight I'd ever recorded. Panic set in. I declared that I had had enough and that I needed to regain control. I'd start the day with a protein shake only to find myself devouring a box of Hot Tamales by lunch. I couldn't seem to regain control.

Positive change only became possible when my approach started to shift from condemnation to curiosity: *Why was I craving sugar and carbs so intensely? What lay behind this sudden change?* Simultaneously, I began to explore my relationship with my weight and my body. What was a genuinely healthy weight? The answer eluded me. I had spent years striving to maintain my weight around 130 pounds, always aiming for even lower. This was connected to my dating life; I believed that I needed to be skinny to be attractive. The fear of loneliness outweighed my desire for junk food and sugar. I avoided indulging to maintain my desired weight. But that motivation was no longer present. Kelly loved my body, period. She didn't love me more when I was skinny. In fact, something revolutionary occurred when I was with her.

Kelly experienced her own cycles of weight loss and gain during our time together. She initially lost weight rapidly, revealing that she wasn't eating much, which concerned me greatly. I didn't want her to skip meals; I didn't find anything attractive about it. As she grappled with her own sugar addiction, her weight increased. Surprisingly, I found her even more attractive. This was a departure from my previous beliefs. Healthy was acquiring a new definition. It became about self-love, and to me, it was more loving to have a little extra weight than to deny oneself. Dieting and restriction no longer seemed like marks of self-control and determination, which I had once admired. Instead, they felt like forms of punishment, which were far from attractive. My entire perception of sexy and healthy was undergoing a transformation. I needed to redefine what I found attractive and determine what I truly wanted for my own body.

When I stepped on the scale one afternoon, my first thought was, *I'm overweight. This is terrible.* Shame crept in, followed by a cascade of self-deprecating thoughts: *I'm disgusting. My belly is filled with rolls and looks awful. Nobody will ever want me. My clothes look terrible on me.* These thoughts haunted me, but were they true? Did I have irrefutable evidence that nobody would love me at this weight? The opposite seemed true. Kelly seemed to love me more. She found me irresistibly sexy with "a little in the middle." I loved that.

My father had been underweight for decades, probably weighing about the same as I did, despite being closer to 5'8" in height compared to my 5'4" stature. I had always admired his skinny physique, but as I examined it more closely, I realized that I found it unattractive. His clothes never seemed to fit properly, and his pants always appeared on the verge of falling off. I also noticed how he perpetually denied himself the foods he secretly craved. He longed to enjoy the spaghetti the rest of us relished but denied himself the carbs. That wasn't the path I wanted to follow.

I had denied myself one thing or another for most of my life, and I was ready to break free from that pattern. I had such a strong desire to experience life in its entirety, which included savoring delicious food. I wanted to relish the taste of cheese on a perfect pizza, savor coffee ice cream from around the world, and take delight in candy, cotton candy, S'mores, and all kinds of sweets and treats. Candy was fun, and I was all about having fun. I wanted to stuff stockings full of gummy Coke bottles and holiday packs of Lifesavers. I longed to revel in all that life had to offer, but how could I reconcile that with an expanding belly? What did I genuinely desire for myself and my family?

My mother served as an inspiring example of what I aspired to achieve: a sense of balance. is one of the most beautiful people I have ever seen, possessing an impeccable fashion sense. She can put together a stunning outfit, even in the midst of a five-day camping trip. On a two-week tour of Italy with just a backpack, she effortlessly conjured new and impressive outfits every day. She can visit REI and emerge with five items, fashioning a hundred different outfits from them. She exudes a sense of fun, cuteness, style, and contentment with her body in every look.

My mom was the embodiment of joy, closely followed by Willy. Both had a way of relishing life and fully immersing themselves in it. They loved food, and they loved travel. They celebrated, indulged, and embraced every moment, and I admired it deeply. I decided it must be all about balance, so I began the work of seeking that balance within myself.

I embarked on a journey of self-trust and self-acceptance, opting for a path free from judgment and criticism. I refrained from using the word "diet" due to its negative connotations, choosing the term "plan" instead. I was on an intuitive plan, a plan rooted in self-trust. Just like learning to ride a bike, finding balance required experiencing moments of imbalance. I was currently in that phase, exploring the side of indulgence. I wasn't just enjoying a few pieces of licorice; I was consuming an entire family-size bag.

It was a period of learning my boundaries and limits. I resigned myself to the fact that I might spend months, years, or even a decade in the same place, honing my understanding of myself and what balance meant for me—then, I would shift back to the other side. Just like riding a bike, the process would entail an ongoing series of micro-adjustments to counterbalance the moments of instability. I aimed to attain the same equilibrium with sugar, food, my belly, and my weight.

All of it would fluctuate as I teetered between indulgence and restraint, but I started to learn how to stop judging the moments of imbalance. I would simply adjust and continue on my journey. I was healing my relationship with food, continuously making micro-corrections and finding joy along the way, savoring all that life had to offer. I was growing accustomed to—and even learning to love—having "a little in the middle."

At the same time that my obsession with sugar intensified, my work ethic seemed to evaporate into thin air. It was as if my superpower of relentless effort and determination had abandoned me when I needed it most. The drive that had propelled me to excel in various areas of my life had vanished, leaving me adrift and lost. It was disorienting and unsettling.

Before my leave of absence, I found myself struggling to focus on my work, particularly my responsibilities at the church. It was a stark departure from my usual dedication and commitment. I had gone from giving my all to doing the bare minimum, and it worried me to no end. The nagging questions haunted me: *Will others be disappointed? Am I letting people down?* I made desperate attempts to force myself into productivity, as if I could simply flip a switch and regain my work ethic. But no matter how hard I tried, I couldn't summon the motivation or concentration to get things done.

Each morning, I'd set lofty goals, promising myself that I would regain control over my tasks and responsibilities.

"Today is the day," I'd declare. "No sugar—and I'm going to power through my emails and write that sermon." But my resolve would crumble within minutes. The mere mention of Kelly in a text message would send me into a daydream, my thoughts consumed by her presence, her voice, her essence. It was as though everything else in my life was fading into the background, overshadowed by my longing for her.

Initially, I perceived this as a temporary hiccup, a pause in my relentless pursuit of achievement that I could make up for later. I justified it by telling myself that I hadn't taken any substantial time off in 30 years—no sabbaticals, no leaves of absence, no extended breaks—so perhaps a week or two now would be acceptable. The workaholic in me struggled to accept this change in my priorities. I was accustomed to putting work and career first, believing that it was the path to success and acceptance. I thought it was the key to belonging.

However, as time went on, I began to realize that this wasn't just a momentary pause. Something fundamental was shifting within me, and my priorities were undergoing a seismic transformation. Love had suddenly surged to the top of my list, an unprecedented occurrence. Never before had I been willing to put someone else above my work. I used to believe that my career should always take precedence, that relationships were secondary. My previous marriages had shown me the consequences of this belief. Prioritizing work wasn't a path to happiness, and I was beginning to see things differently.

The adjustment wasn't easy, though. I grappled with the fear that I was losing my edge, my competitive advantage. *Will I lose it permanently if I don't snap out of this? Will I lose every-thing I've worked so hard to achieve?* I worried about my career and the potential consequences of this shift in my priorities. It felt like I was veering off course, and I couldn't help but fear disappointing everyone.

For most of my life, I had placed work and achievement above all else. It was how I had found my place in the world, how I had earned my spot at the table. I believed that if I ever let up, if I slowed down even for a moment, I would be cast aside. My sense of belonging was contingent on my ability to prove myself, to work tirelessly, and to earn the acceptance of others. I had sacrificed my own well-being and desires in pursuit of this elusive sense of belonging.

But now, as I poured my love into Kelly, something extraordinary was happening. I was rediscovering myself, and in doing so, I was finding a deeper sense of belonging and purpose. This journey was challenging the core of my beliefs. I was learning that belonging didn't come from relentless effort and achievement; it came from authenticity and embracing the fullness of my heart.

I started to see the stark contrast between my old way of life and the new one I was embracing. In the past, I had often forsaken myself to fit in with the expectations of others, prioritizing their needs and desires over my own. But now, I was choosing love and authenticity. I was choosing to put my own needs and desires on equal footing with others'. It was a radical shift in perspective, and it came with its own set of challenges.

As I began to lean into my relationship with Kelly and let love guide my decisions, I felt a spaciousness opening up in my life. It was a space where I could slow down, reassess my path, and reconnect with my true self. It reminded me of the concept that between stimulus and response, there is a space. In this space, I had the opportunity to choose my response rather than reacting impulsively. It was a space of liberation and freedom, and I was beginning to experience it in my life.

My journey into ministry had been marked by a lack of this space. I had been so eager to reach my destination that I had neglected the importance of pausing, reflecting, and discerning.

I had rushed through each step of the process, from seminary to ordination, without taking the time to truly integrate and understand my own calling. It was as if I had been sprinting, never bothering to consult the map or enjoy the scenery along the way.

As I slowed down and allowed myself to be consumed by love, I started to realize the importance of creating that space in my life. I saw the warning signs that I had previously ignored—the yearning for community work and the fear-driven decisions I had made to please others. I had lost sight of the path that had brought me to where I was: on a journey to know myself and deepen my relationship with God.

It became clear that I needed to make a change, to realign with my true calling, even if it meant disappointing others and facing the chaos that came with it. As I confronted the fractures in my life, I recognized that some relationships were based on what I could do for others rather than genuine connection. It was time to rebuild on a foundation of authenticity and love, even if it meant dismantling the structures I had built on sand. I had competing intentions in my life, and it was time to prioritize the ones that truly mattered.

Surely, there was room for balance—room for loving and caring for others while also loving and caring for myself. Throughout my life, what I'd once seen as messes had actually been moments where everything felt like it was falling apart because I'd been trying so hard and had understandably failed to keep everything in balance. From how I appeared to others to whether I did enough, all of those things were overflowing, spilling off the sides of the scale and making a tremendous mess I always felt desperate to clean up.

But now, the mess that had ensued as a result of opening my heart to what I truly wanted was part of the process of shedding my old way of life and stepping into a new, more genuine version of myself. It was a chaotic, often painful journey, but it was also the most liberating and transformative experience of my life. As I leaned into love and allowed myself to be guided by my heart, I began to uncover the magic in the mess, the profound wisdom that comes from coming home to oneself.

Chapter 24

Nashville Calling

During my final days in Eagle, fear stood tall as the dominant force. The fear of falling, failing, and being perceived as a fool clung to me like a dark shadow. I questioned the wisdom of my impending move to Nashville, my leap into the unknown. What if I regretted this choice?

As I delved deeper into my fear, an image emerged of Kelly's tattoos. Among her beautifully inked artistry, one quote on her forearm captured my attention: "What if I fall? Oh, but my darling, what if you fly?" These words, originally written by poet Erin Hanson, resonated deeply. It addressed my current fears and encapsulated the essence of stepping beyond one's comfort zone to embrace risk. As it said so clearly, our reluctance to act often stemmed from the fear of failure—but I was realizing that facing fear and acting in spite of it was a marker of being all-in.

I sat at the kitchen table in the parsonage in my favorite seat, the one right in the middle of the afternoon sunbeam. Otis plodded toward me and put his face on my knee. I felt his uncertainty and longed to be able to give him answers about what was next. I glanced around the room, most of it empty. So much letting go had taken place in this liminal space. As I sat in the sunbeam, taking in all the work I had done to get this place packed up, a story I remembered flashed through my mind.

Some climbers were attempting an uncharted route, and they reached a point where retreating wasn't an option; they had to commit 100 percent. The ropes they carried wouldn't allow them to descend after ascending a certain pitch. They had to make an all-in choice, and they went on to make history. Some leaps of faith were like that, leaving no room for turning back—a terrifying yet transformative experience.

In retrospect, I understood how far from being all-in I had been in past relationships. I always ensured that there was an escape route. Whether in cohabitation or marriage, having an out in case things went awry had seemed prudent. This pattern led to not one but two divorces, as well as plenty of surface-level relationships. How could I truly invest when I constantly kept one foot on the platform, ready to retreat? Deep, spiritual connections remained elusive because I feared the intensity and commitment required. I yearned for profound connections while shying away from fully embracing them.

There were no exit strategies, backup plans, or emotional

safety nets in my relationship with Kelly—no other emotional relationships to fall back on if heartbreak ensued, and no alternate job to bury myself in if I faced rejection or devastation. Yet, I was still taking the plunge and risking it all. I was finally embracing being all-in.

What had shifted? Why now? Why was I fully committed to this relationship while others had left me on the fence? For the first time, I found myself more interested in the possibility of soaring than dwelling on the fear of falling. In the past, the fear of failure had always overshadowed the potential reward. Embracing the risk, the possibility of failure, became the price of admission to something truly extraordinary.

As I shut off all the lights and walked up the stairs to my bedroom, Otis trailed behind me. I still had a few things left unpacked in this room, and it was the one place in the house that still felt livable. I brushed my teeth, threw on a T-shirt, and hopped into bed. Otis hopped onto the mattress beside me and nestled under the covers. I loved feeling him snuggle up against me—it was something I could count on.

As I lay there with the lights out, I recalled the late nights of endless debates with my ex-husband, unable to decide whether to commit or walk away. We had broken up repeatedly, stuck in a cycle of indecision. I'd craved a partner, a family, and stability but had struggled to find the right fit. I'd questioned if I was impossible to be around or too set in my ways. Our solution had been separate homes, each living in a different county. I'd justified it as an introverted need for solitude. In reality, it was a sign of a mismatched partnership.

With Kelly, everything felt different. Being apart was unbearable; we even coined the term "E.T. sick" to describe our intense connection. Like E.T. and Elliott, we shared emotions and energies across distances. It was as though her feelings became mine, and it was challenging to distinguish whose emotions were whose. Despite the difficulties of such a connection, I couldn't imagine being without it. When we were apart, my energy dwindled, and longing consumed me. I felt incomplete without her, a sensation I'd never experienced before. The trade-off was worth it—I was more focused on the joy of loving her than the fear of rejection.

Too often, I considered, we fixated on the prospect of failure instead of dreaming of success. What did "flying" really look like for each of us? Was it pursuing a new hobby, asking someone out, traveling, or seeking an unanswered prayer?

Flying with Kelly meant considering unprecedented possibilities. When I discussed the prospect of moving to Nashville, it felt less like a choice and more like destiny. I yearned for partnership, family, and a sense of belonging. but in the past, my reluctance to fully commit had hindered those desires.

The fear of disappointing others and the need to maintain a façade of stability had held me back. My sense of obligation to my church—and even more significantly, my fear of disappointing my father—had trapped me in Eagle. My fear of taking the next step, of asking for a leave of absence and moving to Nashville, exposed the truth—I was driven by fear and obligation rather than love. The weight of my sense of duty was holding me captive. But finally, I was acknowledging that my heart and intuition were guiding me elsewhere. I needed to be with Kelly; there was no other option.

I had to make the difficult choice to tell my parents about my plan to take a leave of absence and move to Nashville sooner than expected. This decision was driven by authenticity, a return to my true path, and an unwavering love for Kelly. The sands of inauthenticity were being washed away, and I was rebuilding my life on a solid foundation, one day at a time, with Kelly by my side.

Every aspect of my life was transforming, from my under-standing of sexuality and gender to my calling, career, family, and friendships. It was a whirlwind of self-discovery and growth, sometimes overwhelming but always rewarding. I sought self-improvement relentlessly, investing time and resources to uncover my blind spots. With Kelly's insight and unwavering honesty, I couldn't hide from the truth. I was fine-tuning my life and letting go of the sand, building my founda-tion upon the rock of authenticity.

It wasn't easy, but I knew that the liberation, joy, and love on the other side of this journey would be worth every hardship. If it were easy, everyone would do it. I was willing to face the hard truths and do the work—for love, and for the future that awaited us.

Chapter 25

A Lesbian Retreat

In the midst of my newfound love, I grappled with a sense of loneliness that seemed contradictory. Coming out had become a multifaceted journey, far more complex than merely accepting my own identity and navigating others' reactions. It was an unearthing of every unresolved issue in my life, a profound cleansing of my very existence. Like an exhaustive cleaning of a cluttered room, I examined every relationship, shaking out the dust and asking each person, "Do you choose to know this authentic version of me?" This process forced me to confront my own self-worth and authenticity.

Before I could extend this to others, I realized that I had to undergo the same process with myself. I had to scrutinize every aspect of my life, from my beliefs to my clothes, reevaluating how I perceived acceptance, achievement, gender, and partnership. It was like reconstructing my entire existence from the ground up. Despite the seismic shift it triggered, this transformation was also the cathartic purging I had longed for—it was a personal growth program on steroids. I had assumed I had done substantial self-work before, but this journey revealed there was so much more I didn't even know I didn't know.

As I reevaluated my entire life through the lens of my newfound identity as a gay woman, I began to see everything differently. Past events, like the first boy-girl party where I shied away from kissing games, took on new meaning. I questioned why I had played rugby in college and why my previous marriages had failed. I felt like I was replaying the movie of my life with a different ending, and I suddenly understood things that had previously baffled me. It was like the lights had been turned on, illuminating the relationships between different aspects of my life. The result was greater compassion for myself; I appreciated the reasons behind my choices and actions.

Amidst this profound self-exploration and transformation, I felt incredibly isolated. It appeared to everyone that I was changing, that something new was happening to me, but in reality, I was just embracing my true self. I had built my world on a flawed image of who I was, and that world was crumbling. I hadn't truly known myself, and the revelation was overwhelming. The questions swirled: *How had I not realized I was gay? How had I veered so far from my true gender expression? How had I lost my way in life?* I was drowning in uncertainty, and I needed support.

That support materialized in the form of what I affectionately called the "Lesbian Retreat," officially known as the

Bloomers Society—a group for late bloomers who came out later in life. Kelly had found a coach to help her navigate this journey and had initially planned to attend the retreat alone. However, I was grappling with so much—friends dying of cancer, moving away from the only home I'd ever known, and all the other tumultuous changes in my life that I realized I needed the support and community as well. So, I decided to join her.

I dove headfirst into the retreat without fully understanding what it entailed. I simply knew I needed support during this period of upheaval and change. The retreat spanned from Friday evening through Sunday, and it was designed primarily for women who had been married to men before coming out as lesbians later in life—perfect for me, who had been in two previous marriages and was embarking on this journey at the age of forty-seven.

I met Kelly in Nashville and, together, we packed up the car. As we arrived at the airport parking lot, excitement and anticipation filled the air. We had four uninterrupted days ahead of us, just the two of us, and we were about to meet other couples facing similar challenges. We parked the car, and I felt a surge of confidence and a newfound sense of masculinity—something I had never experienced in previous relationships. I was determined to take care of Kelly and make this trip unforgettable.

We kissed passionately in the parking lot, savoring every moment together. As I retrieved our luggage, handed Kelly her backpack, and closed the trunk, a sudden realization hit me— Kelly's roller bag was missing.

"Wait, your bag!" I said helplessly, panic and confusion gripping my insides.

Kelly had a strange expression on her face as she realized she had left her bag at home. She plainly said as much, and my heart sank, thinking this was the end of our much-anticipated trip. I thought she must be furious with me. Eric would have made this my fault because, of course, *I* hadn't made sure all the bags were in the car. Growing up in a family where one kid being in trouble meant all of us were in trouble had led to this habit of assuming blame, a hard habit to break.

However, Kelly's response surprised me. She didn't seem upset at all. In fact, she was remarkably calm about the situation. She said we'd simply have to go shopping to replace what she had left behind. Her nonchalant attitude caught me off guard.

"Do you want to go back and get it?" I asked, bewildered.

"Of course not! There's no time. It's no big deal," she replied.

I was astonished by her reaction. She had forgotten her bag, with all her clothes, toiletries, and essentials, yet she wasn't fazed in the slightest.

"Are you mad?" she asked me in the silence that followed.

Confusion clouded my thoughts. "Am I mad? Why? No, of course not. Are you mad?"

"Oh my gosh, no. This happens to me all the time! I'm worried this is upsetting to you, and you'll think I'm a total flake," she admitted.

I assured her that her oversight didn't upset me in the least, but I was amazed at her composure. We were both relieved that this hiccup hadn't ruined our trip. It was a revelation, a stark contrast to my past relationships, where such incidents had the power to derail entire vacations.

Our hotel room in Houston was located inside a mall, an unexpected surprise. Kelly quickly found clothes for the weekend, and we replaced her toiletries during a quick stop at Target. It seemed like a fortunate turn of events, an opportunity to see a molehill for what it was rather than the insurmountable, relationship-rocking mountain it would've been with anybody else. Maybe I didn't need to be perfect with Kelly. Maybe it was okay to not have everything figured out.

The retreat, while not what I had initially expected, proved to be a profoundly impactful experience. Each participant had the opportunity to share their coming out story, and I realized the immense power of both listening to others' stories and sharing our own. It made me feel heard and seen, like I was part of a community in ways I had never been before.

Themes emerged throughout the weekend, highlighting the challenges many faced when coming out later in life. It was clear that some had discovered their true selves and desires after entering into marriages, starting careers, and creating families. The pain of living inauthentically, of denying one's true identity, was excruciating. Many participants had tried to maintain their existing lives while also grappling with their newfound attraction to the same gender. It was complex and emotionally agonizing for them in that liminal space, torn between a life they loved and their longing for something more.

As I listened to these heart-wrenching stories, I felt compassion for everyone who was trying to live a life that no longer resonated with their authentic self. I also felt grateful that I had separated from my marriage before fully embracing my true identity. Often, the process of coming out gets tangled with the process of separation and divorce, creating additional layers of pain and confusion.

The experience highlighted the pressing need for more open and honest conversations about self-discovery, personal growth, and the journey to knowing one's true self. It raised critical questions about the institution of marriage and whether it should be more adaptable to accommodate the evolving identities and desires of individuals. It reinforced the idea that our lives should be an ongoing quest for self-understanding, learning, and transformation, where we have the freedom to explore, evolve, and authentically redefine ourselves without fear or judgment.

Ultimately, it emphasized the profound richness that came from embracing one's true self and living in alignment with one's genuine desires—an affirmation of the age-old wisdom to "know thyself" and "to thine own self be true."

Chapter 26

All-In

I sat at the kitchen table at the parsonage, trying my best not to succumb to panic. I'd driven Otis and a carload of stuff to Nashville a few weeks earlier, so half of my belongings were in Nashville, and the other half were in Eagle. It felt fitting, as I was torn between the two places. I felt the pull of this new adventure with Kelly, in a new city with new possibilities. But with the door closed on ministry, my marriage, and the church, the road to opportunity was wide open—even if there was a lot to leave behind. My emotions ranged from excitement and exhilaration to trepidation and grief. I was all over the place, much like my stuff.

As I gazed at the serene snowfall through the kitchen window, my thoughts darted around inside my head. *Will the pile of stuff in the living room fit in the car? What happens if it doesn't? What will I leave behind? Will my beloved plants survive the journey to Nashville? I'll have to bring them into the hotel with me; I can't leave them in the car! I miss Otis. At least the plants won't need restroom breaks on the way.*

This was the precipice of panic, where the familiar and the unknown collided. I had called Colorado home for most of my life, with only a brief four-year hiatus on the coast of Maine during college. For forty-three years, I had remained within a 250-mile radius of this state. Eagle County had been my home for the past thirteen years. Colorado was my comfort zone, a place I'd grown, stumbled, and thrived. But even comfort can become uncomfortable when it starts to stifle your growth.

While the prospect of this new chapter in Nashville was undeniably exciting, it was also incredibly daunting. Leaving behind the place I'd always known, the community I'd become a part of, and the familiarity of my daily life was nothing short of terrifying. I was saying goodbye to the post office where they knew my name, to the reassuring presence of familiar faces wherever I went, to my friends, my parents, my job, and a substantial portion of my possessions. Embarking on this journey was downright scary.

Meanwhile, in Nashville, I knew just three people. I lacked job security, and I was clueless about Tennessee. As I dissected my fears, it became evident that two significant components were at play: a sense of belonging and the comfort of knowing.

I felt a profound sense of belonging in Colorado—or so I thought. People recognized me, and I felt like a vital thread in the community's tapestry. It had taken years to cultivate this sense of belonging—I held it dear and feared how deeply I would miss it. But I would come to understand that what I thought was belonging was actually just a façade. Belonging wasn't about how many people knew my name or liked me, it was about being true to myself. And it was in Nashville, where I knew next to no one, that I truly felt a sense of belonging.

I was familiar with life in Colorado, from the towns and running trails to the weather patterns. I'd understood my purpose and the role I was meant to play in this environment. The puzzle pieces of my vision were clearer here, allowing me to grasp how they fit together. Now, I was venturing into the unknown, essentially forcing myself to grapple with profound uncertainty.

It wasn't that I felt like I was looking at an incomplete puzzle; rather, it was as though I only possessed one puzzle piece. This seemed to be how the universe operated with me— providing me with one piece at a time. It reminded me of Indiana Jones in *The Last Crusade*, taking that leap of faith across the abyss without seeing the entire bridge beforehand. That first step into the unknown required something extraordinary.

As I peered into the unknown, all my fears rushed to the surface. What if I fell? What if I failed? What if there was nothing waiting for me on the other side? On the other hand, what if there was a treasure waiting—the Holy Grail of my life's purpose? At this point, all I could see was the next step in my journey: completing my job at UMC of Eagle Valley, packing my car (as much as it could hold), and making my way back to Nashville. Beyond that lay a vast expanse of the unknown. I didn't know what awaited me in Nashville, how I would serve, who I would meet, or what kind of life lay ahead.

In the midst of this fear, I chose to believe. I went for the magic. I chose trust. I chose faith. This was where I found my footing. Deep in my heart, I sensed a calling to Nashville. I'd felt it long before my relationship with Kelly came into the picture—a mysterious tug, a whisper from the divine, an intuition nudging me toward this city. Regardless of the words I use to describe it—being called by God, answering a divine call, hearing the still small voice, following intuition, or feeling nudged—I was resolute in my belief that I was called.

I would take the leap, with faith as my wings and trust as my compass. I'd leaped before—quitting jobs that weren't the right fit, authoring a book, diving into suicide prevention, and embracing ministry. Each leap had required courage, and each jump had propelled me into uncharted territory, but every time I landed, I'd uncovered a world that surpassed my wildest dreams. As I often said, "It was more than I knew to dream of." With each calling, the leaps grew larger, the jumps higher, and the faith required deeper. Now, the greatest leap of my life awaited me, and I stood at the edge, equal parts terrified and exhilarated.

There was a part of me that embraced the messiness of these leaps, delighted in the chaos, and reveled in the breakdown of the familiar order of life. The rhythm of dismantling, shedding the old, and reshaping my world to see myself, others, and the universe with fresh, loving eyes felt addictive. I kept taking these leaps, free-falling into the unknown, crashing, gathering the pieces, and reassembling them, only to leap again.

This process had unfolded in Eagle, where I'd thought I had figured it all out. I had completed seminary, had been on the cusp of becoming an ordained elder in the United Methodist Church, and had a fulfilling appointment in a faith community I cherished. It was a picture-perfect moment with all the pieces fitting together seamlessly: speaking, writing, working with children, learning, and finding meaning and purpose centered on faith. To top it off, I had gotten married, adding what I'd thought would be the final piece to my life's puzzle. But it had been an illusion. My marriage had crumbled, and my role in ministry had cracked. I had struggled with vows of celibacy until marriage, and the compromises required felt contrary to being true to myself. I had been asked to forsake aspects of my identity to fit into the mold of ministry. It had almost completed it, but it hadn't held together.

For eight years, I had tried to force the pieces of ministry into place, just as I had done with my marriage. I had fought hard, thinking that sheer determination could make it work. I had been exhausted, pretending, and using all my energy to hold it together. These pieces hadn't fit, and it was time to let go and honor my truth, the truth that would guide me to the completed puzzle.

I stared at the pile of photo frames, records, and empty planters sticking out of the pile by the door like splinters and sighed. Quitting my marriage had carried a weighty burden of shame and guilt. I had felt like a fraud and a failure, letting everyone down, including myself. But deep down, I knew that honoring my truth was the path to finding the missing pieces of my puzzle.

I was taking the leap, despite its weight. I would leave Eagle and allow all the pieces to fall. Finally, I was going to speak my truth, and I wouldn't have to force the pieces to fit anymore. I had stopped pretending, and for the first time, I was not disappointed at the end of the day. I stood on the precipice, ready to leap into the unknown in Nashville, with faith as my wings and trust as my compass. It was a leap that would lead me to a deeper, more loving relationship with myself, with Kelly, and with the world around me. It was a leap that would teach me that sometimes, we must first let go of what we know to be true to find new ways of seeing, believing, and living.

I was following my heart, even if it meant risking everything. For the first time, I was all-in.

Chapter 27

Becoming Unapologetically Me

Moving to Nashville didn't come without its bumps. I left more things behind than I cared to: my Denver Broncos gear, my lawn chairs, and half of my Christmas decorations. It was "out with the old" in so many ways. I left Colorado on a high and skidded into Nashville overwhelmed by fear. Just as my plane landed in Tennessee, the weight of it all hit me: *What am I doing? I don't know anyone here. I'm all alone.* I couldn't wait to grab onto Kelly and remember the why of all of this.

The Uber pulled into the driveway of the home Kelly had recently purchased in East Nashville. She and Lucy had moved in quickly at Thanksgiving, and I knew there was a lot to do to make it home for the three of us. I walked up the driveway and saw a light on in the bedroom. My heart ached with anticipation. This was my home, with her. I got out and immediately heard Otis at the door. *My boy!* I opened the door and Otis wrestled me to the ground with nudges, wiggles, and kisses. I grabbed him hard and held on.

I breathed him in, the way I did during so many late-night desperations. *He is here, this is home, I'm okay.* I got up and went to the bedroom to find Kelly asleep with her glasses on her face, book in her lap, and her dog, Olive, curled up by her side. She took my breath away. This was my girl.

I leaned over and kissed her cheek. She startled awake. I reached down and gave her a huge hug. I held onto her, shaking with nerves and fatigue from the long day of travel. As I held her in my arms, she began to sob. "Oh, my love," I said as I held onto her. "What is it?"

Kelly couldn't talk; she just sobbed harder. I just held her as she melted into me. Kelly shared her struggles with her ex and how alone she had felt. On top of it all, she felt incredibly sick— sore throat, sore muscles, and achy all over. She remained in bed for the next three days while Otis and I unpacked everything I had moved so far. Just when I had everything put away, Kelly emerged a new human being. We began the process of creating a home, living together, and sharing this life.

A few months later, my brother came to visit us, and I had been counting down the days until he arrived. Finally, I was going to have a familiar face in Nashville. While I wanted Willy to stay in our office, I acquiesced that it would indeed be too tight a squeeze. We rented him and his wife a tiny home about a mile away. The house was adorable, and it gave us all a bit of space. Kelly and Willy hit it off right away. They nerded out over recipes and making ribs on the grill. They cooked up a storm while my sister-in-law helped me put together shelves, fill picture frames, and complete other moving projects I hadn't yet gotten to.

The giddiness I felt for Willy's arrival was more than just excitement; he felt like a beacon of familiarity in a city still new to me. His presence underscored a stark truth: I'd been feeling alone. Creating a home with Kelly and Lucy had been wonderful, yet the absence of familiar faces hit hard. His visit was like sunshine for my soul.

One afternoon, we were all taking a break from housework when Willy retreated to the back deck. I walked out and found him reclining on the outdoor couch with Otis snuggled next to him. He was under the shade with a large glass of ice water and his book propped on his chest. As his eyes danced down the page, he looked so relaxed, so happy, so at peace. I looked at him longingly—I so badly wished to feel that way again too.

When it was time to drop Willy and his wife off at the airport, I found myself overwhelmed with emotion. Watching them walk through the sliding doors to return home, I felt the weight of all the recent changes in my life. I'd spent years conforming to expectations, squeezing into a metaphorical box that never quite fit, and now I was in the process of stepping out of that box. Staring after Willy at the airport, I mourned for lost time, for the suppressed parts of myself, and the deep ache for family and authenticity. Every day was an opportunity for me to rediscover myself, to reclaim what fit for my life.

The next day, inspired by watching Willy read on the back

porch, I bought a new book and sank into it. It was an unantici-
pated joy that felt like reuniting with an old friend. I devoured a
book in two days, a feat I hadn't achieved in months. This return
to joy was a reminder of the person I'd always been, buried
under the chaos of transformation.

Even as I worked to recover the lost parts of myself that
had always been present, there were other parts of me that
were new and different. I noticed myself responding differently in tricky situations. One afternoon, Kelly mentioned she
needed to meet with Rick. She often needed to talk with him—
about Lucy and logistics—and for months, this brought me to
boiling. I understood, but Kelly sharing that she missed him,
wanted to see him, or anything of that nature triggered me
instantly. I felt things I was accustomed to—anger, jealousy,
fear.

Prior to that afternoon, suggesting a meetup with Rick
would have triggered a whirlwind of jealousy and insecurity.
But this time, I responded with compassion and even suggested
they meet at our home. This shift from turmoil to tranquility
marked a profound healing. I was learning to find peace amid
what once caused chaos.

I made myself comfortable at the coffee shop just down the
road from our house. I could now navigate my way there
without using Google Maps, which felt like a huge victory. I
ordered myself an English breakfast tea with coconut and
almond milk. I found a two-top in the back next to an outlet. I
pulled my laptop out of my backpack and plugged it in. For the
first time in a very long time, I felt settled enough to enjoy

sitting down with a cup of tea to write. I felt at home in a way I never had before—at home inside myself.

Driving back to the house from the coffee shop, I caught myself heading down a familiar road, catastrophizing about Kelly and Rick. I hadn't been triggered when Kelly mentioned wanting to meet with Rick, or for the last few hours when I knew they were meeting in our home. And yet, as I headed back to the house, I felt the familiar thoughts of insecurity. I envisioned walking in to find them in a deep embrace, kissing, and then receiving the news that they were getting back together.

I began to live the sting of rejection, loss, and fear. I felt the pangs of losing Kelly in every cell of my body and felt my muscles tighten and my stomach churn. And then I caught myself. *What am I doing?* I thought. *Why am I creating this for myself? Why am I torturing myself like this?*

"No more," I declared to myself in the car—and just like that, I stopped. My peace returned, and I found myself smiling at the ridiculousness of how much energy I had used creating this fictionalized hell. I was so adept at creating my own fantasy, so why not create something awesome? I shook my head at the silliness of it all. With a bit more altitude, I could see how much pain and suffering I'd caused myself trying to prepare for the worst. What I was actually doing was living the worst, all the time. I didn't want to do that to myself anymore.

As I approached the house, I noticed Rick's truck was still in the driveway. I smiled. It was fascinating to me how quickly all the suffering had vanished. I felt love for Kelly, compassion for the space she was in, and a deep space in my heart for Rick. We were all connected. This was our new blended family, and he was becoming a huge part of my life, as Kelly's best friend, Lucy's dad, and now, for me, family.

Moving to Nashville, getting kicked out of the church, coming out, losing myself, and and finding myself again—it was all so tumultuous, but it was invaluable. I discovered a more authentic version of myself, one that found belonging not in pleasing others but in being unapologetically me. In the mess of it all, I found the ability to embrace chaos as a catalyst for transformation—and a deeper capacity to love.

I learned that real peace isn't about avoiding turmoil but finding serenity within it, in the power of self-compassion and the beauty of embracing life's imperfections. In every challenge, there was an opportunity for growth—and in every mess, there was magic waiting to be discovered.

Chapter 28

Beyond Expectations

S ome things grab my laser-like focus, while others slip through my awareness almost unnoticed. I struggle daily to make sense of which is which, but the answer usually eludes me. As we embarked on a journey to Pittsburgh to drop Lucy off at camp with her cousins, my primary concerns were ensuring our safe arrival and carving out time for my writing. We would stop at Kelly's parents' house to visit and then drive up with her sister and Lucy's cousin the rest of the way to the camp in Ohio. I diligently plugged Kelly's parents' address in Pittsburgh into the app on my phone and regularly checked the remaining miles and estimated arrival time. Whenever the numbers aligned in a quirky way, like "111 miles to the next turn" or "arrival at 4:44 PM," I couldn't resist announcing them aloud, finding peculiar satisfaction in these numerical coincidences.

Conversely, our plans for the upcoming week seemed to float in the distance, nebulous and dreamlike. While Lucy was at camp, Kelly and I were going on a little getaway ourselves. I knew we had accommodations lined up somewhere near Shenandoah National Park, but the exact location on the map and the state it belonged to didn't occupy my thoughts. My mind fixated on the journey—the miles to conquer and the impending arrival—while the broader itinerary barely registered.

The journey stretched ahead, a three-hour drive that felt daunting after my recent escapades. I had just navigated a U-Haul from Breckenridge to Eagle to Nashville to bring a load of my things to the house, and was now back in the driver's seat, steering us from Nashville to Pittsburgh for our visit with Kelly's family, then Ohio for camp, and finally to Shenandoah River for some time away, just the two of us. Despite my road-weariness, I was excited for an adventure with Kelly, though I couldn't help but notice that I'd neglected the trip's logistics. *Why had I been so detached from the planning? When had Kelly arranged everything? How am I so out of the loop?*

About an hour from our intended destination, we pulled into a country store replete with cider, puzzles, and other cabin essentials. It was then that thoughts of our upcoming days crept into my consciousness. I envisioned a rustic cabin deep in the woods with a roaring fire, crocheted blankets, steaming mugs of hot chocolate, and soft cuddles. The store's shelves were stocked with cabin delights, and I could feel my excitement building. My instinct nudged me toward buying a puzzle, but I knew that my obsessive nature would lead me to relentlessly focus on its completion—a less-than-ideal way to spend our limited time together. Instead, I opted for a few ears of corn, a bag of peaches, a homegrown tomato, and a fresh loaf of banana nut bread.

As the miles rolled away and the estimated arrival time loomed closer, the landscape became increasingly captivating. Rolling hills and lush green valleys stretched before us. We made a left turn, and according to my phone, the Iris Inn awaited just up ahead. The name caught my attention—this "inn" sounded far more luxurious than the cabin I had envisioned. I brushed aside my reservations, refusing to overthink it, and made the left turn up the hill. Shock awaited me—this was no rustic cabin; it was an upscale destination!

Each cabin stood perched on a steep hill on stilts, with most of the structure suspended above the ground. They resembled treehouses, boasting stunning walls of glass windows and sliding doors, each with a deck that extended into the surrounding trees. They were breathtaking.

As we approached the main lodge, my gaze was drawn to the view. The pristine white building overlooked a sprawling valley, its lawns and flower beds meticulously manicured. It promised an unparalleled vantage point for savoring sunsets, with hammocks, porch swings, and lawn chairs thoughtfully placed for optimum enjoyment. Fire pits were prepared as well; those that weren't gas-powered were stacked with firewood and lighters nearby, all ready to go.

We parked the car in front of the lodge, and as Kelly

stepped out, we both absorbed the tranquil surroundings. The warm air carried a sweet scent, a refreshing departure from the confines of the car. The unexpected turn from what I initially imagined as a rustic cabin into a luxurious retreat intensified my excitement. I couldn't wait to explore this new environment, settle into our upscale Vrbo, and savor every moment of our adventure. The Iris Inn was a five-star escape, and I couldn't wait to make the most of it.

Inside the main lodge, the gift shop beckoned with spa items, white robes, and souvenirs celebrating luxury stays. My inner desires danced with delight at the sight of these tempting offerings. I was eager to indulge in the spa basket and any other luxuries the Inn had in store.

This unexpected twist in our journey—from my rustic cabin expectation to a luxurious escape—deepened my appreciation for the adventure. It reminded me that life sometimes surprises us with the extraordinary when we least expect it. As Kelly and I prepared to embrace this new experience, I couldn't help but feel engaged, not only in the trip itself but also in the evolving adventure of our life together.

We checked in, received the keys, and headed to our cabin. My mind struggled to keep up, transitioning from rustic expectations to the reality of this pristine inn. I wondered what lay ahead, my expectations already exceeded.

I turned the key in the door, not entirely sure what to expect. The room took me by surprise. Rose petals adorned the bed, champagne glasses were filled with non-alcoholic sparkling wine, chocolates tempted us from the counter, bathrobes hung invitingly, and a spa kit beckoned. I was in heaven. The bed boasted the softest white sheets, and I couldn't help but think how amazing this stay would be. I slid open the glass door, revealing our private balcony with a breathtaking view. Beyond that, a private hot tub awaited—naked hot tubbing was in my future.

I completed a thorough scan of the room and noticed that Kelly had ordered dinner, beautifully arranged on the table in front of the fireplace and illuminated by candlelight. What had I done to deserve this? I felt special, a feeling that had so often eluded me in the past. For much of my life, I had found things underwhelming, focusing on flaws and rarely feeling entirely satisfied. The notion of being special had always seemed just out of reach. Yet here it was, drenching me like a firehose, and I felt truly special, far beyond anything I could have imagined wanting. The surprises just kept coming.

Kelly and I enjoyed sandwiches, fruit, crackers, and cheese in front of the fire. We joked about my earlier expectation of hot dogs and chips, reminiscing about this crazy journey. We recalled our first cabin experience, reflecting on how far we'd come since then—it felt both like yesterday and a lifetime ago. We watched the sun set, took a dip in the hot tub, and couldn't stop touching each other. Finally, we made our way to the bed and made love. It was an orgasmic experience unlike anything I had ever felt before. It just kept coming, and I rolled around on the bed in pure ecstasy. It might sound like a storybook ending, but I couldn't fabricate this. It was the best sex of my life, and I knew that there was still much more to come.

We fell into a deep sleep, a natural outcome of such intense pleasure. We awoke before the sun. Just as we began to stir, Kelly whispered in my ear, "I have an idea. Let's drive to the park and watch the sunrise." I couldn't contain my love for this woman—her spontaneity thrilled me.

"Yes!" was my emphatic response to the kind of adventure I typically encouraged in others.

We grabbed some hot tea, donned sweatshirts, and set off for the park. We were ahead of the sun, the perfect timing for our sunrise escapade.

Kelly motioned for me to pull into the first scenic overlook in Shenandoah National Park. I started to park but was surprised when she said, "No, back in." Backing into a pull-through, one-way scenic spot wasn't exactly straightforward.

I questioned, "But won't I block the turnout?"

Her response intrigued me.

"So what?" she asked. "Do it."

I was taken aback—where had this assertiveness come from? I liked it, but it was unexpected. I went for it, seizing the entire space. I backed in, and Kelly hopped out of the car and went around to the trunk, opening it and beckoning me to follow. She had arranged pillows and soft blankets in the trunk, the perfect spot to watch the sunrise.

"Come snuggle with me," she invited. I obliged, finding solace in her embrace. This girl had an incredible effect on me. We sat there, wrapped in warm blankets, feeling the cold nip at our cheeks, holding each other, and waiting for the sunrise. It couldn't get any better; it was perfect.

My cheek rested against hers, her arms providing a cocoon of love and support. I never wanted to move from that spot. "I got you something," she whispered into my ear.

Confused, I asked, "What?" How could there possibly be more? I was already over the moon.

She reached into her backpack and pulled out a box. *Is that a jewelry box? No, wait, a ring box? Is she proposing?* She opened the box with one hand to reveal the most beautiful ring fashioned out of wood with a thin strip of rose gold through the center. It was stunning. Kelly began to reflect on our love story before turning to look in my eyes.

"Will you marry me?" she asked. My heart raced, a million thoughts running through my mind. Was this happening? The emotions surged, and all I could do was cry. I cried and smiled at her, overwhelmed by the intensity of joy. *How did I reach this point?* I thought. *How had I become so fortunate?* She held my hands as I cried and smiled, at a complete loss for words.

After a few moments and with a smile, she added, "Is that a yes?" I laughed and nodded.

"Yes," I muttered as my voice returned, growing in volume until it was a shout. "Yes—hell yes! Fuck yes!"

Kelly placed the ring on my finger and held onto me tightly. "I'm going to marry you," she whispered into my ear. Yes, I was going to marry the love of my life. Soon, I would have a wife.

I couldn't believe how everything was falling into place. While I had been married twice before, I had never been proposed to. I had never been surprised in this way, treated with such tenderness, thoughtfulness, and care. Her generosity of spirit was unlike anything I had experienced before, and the thought of a lifetime with her was beyond my wildest dreams. This was a fairy tale, a true fairy tale, and it was my life. Was I dreaming? I didn't care—either way, this was extraordinary. I was engaged!

As the first light of dawn painted the sky in hues of orange and pink, and the warmth of Kelly's embrace enveloped me, I couldn't help but feel that every mess in life had brought me to this beautiful, unexpected moment. With the ring on my finger and tears of joy in our eyes, we embraced the promise of a lifetime together, filled with love, adventure, and endless possibilities. Our engagement was not just a symbol of our commitment but also a testament to the magic we had discovered in the mess of life, reminding us that sometimes the most extraordinary moments are born out of unexpected twists and turns.

Epilogue
Perfect Imperfection

As I penned the final chapter of this journey, a profound realization dawned on me: the magic of life isn't in perfection, but in the beautiful chaos of being true to oneself. I reflected on my unique talents, especially my penchant for recalling movie quotes, and I chuckled. Though seemingly trivial, to me, that reaction symbolizes my journey to self-acceptance. It reminds me that embracing our quirks means embracing our true selves, no matter how unconventional they might be.

Sitting at my desk, I felt a wave of contentment wash over me. The journey of writing this book mirrored my own path to self-discovery. Each chapter flowed from my heart, narrating not just my story, but the universal tale of finding oneself amid life's mess. The destination, I realized, was never the goal; it was about embracing every twist, turn, and bump along the way.

The quote, "It was a good dream," from *The Man Without*

a Face echos in my thoughts, but it is more than just a line from a favorite movie. To me, it symbolizes the dreams we all hold dear—of love, success, and happiness—though often, these dreams lead us down paths we never expected. In my life, the pursuit led through highs and lows, to love and self-discovery. As I reflect on my own "good dream," I am grateful it brought me to a loving partner, a joyful child, and a life filled with laughter and love.

However, another realization followed that hit me in a burst of clarity: the life that I had always dreamt of could always have already been mine. It was never a distant goal but a reality I could shape with my choices and the courage to be my authentic self. I made it here by embracing life's messiness, by learning from my mistakes, and by daring to be true to myself.

This journey taught me that perfection is an illusion. True fulfillment comes from embracing our authentic selves, with all our quirks, flaws, and idiosyncrasies. It's about letting go of the relentless pursuit of being everything to everyone and finding joy in being unapologetically you. My true path wasn't about conforming to others' expectations but honoring my wonderfully imperfect self.

As I close this chapter, both in my book and in life, I extend an invitation to you: embrace the magic in your mess. Find joy in your imperfections, strength in your vulnerabilities, and happiness in being your true self. Remember that the magic isn't "out there" in a perfect, unattainable life—it's right *here*, in the beautifully chaotic journey of becoming authentically you.

As you turn the pages, remember to celebrate your uniqueness and to find the magic in every beautiful moment. The journey doesn't end here; it's just the beginning. Embrace your mess, and let the magic unfold.

In my life, my divorce was not a conclusion but a the onset of transformation. The echoes of my resilience through the failures reminded me, once again, that every stumble was an opportunity for growth. When I embraced it, my vulnerability became a source of strength. In the quiet surrender to my own authenticity, I found the magic in my own mess and the hidden learnings in my own perceived failures.

As I wipe away the tears and stand at the intersection of my past and an uncertain future, I am still on that journey. As the echoes of society's judgments fade from my mind, I can feel them being replaced by the empowering resonance of my own voice. I am not defined by my failures but by my strength to rise from them.

With that perspective, the intersection becomes a crossroads of possibilities where I can choose the path that best aligns with my true self—the a path less traveled and often obscured by societal expectations and personal insecurities, but uniquely mine. Now, I step into the unknown guided by an inner compass that whispers with authenticity and self-love instead of self-doubt. The road ahead may still be uncertain, but in the chaos, I now see an opportunity for rebirth.

As I move forward, I am not on a quest to escape any failures but to celebrate resilience and self-discovery. As the sun sets on the landscape of my past, I welcome the darkness as a canvas for a new dawn, and the alchemy of transformation begins. I carry all the lessons of my messy magic into the chapters of my life that are yet to unfold— I hope that you will do the same.

Acknowledgments

First and foremost, to my family:

Mom: Thank you for showing me the magic and power in my femininity and what it means to be a true leader. Your strength and grace have been my guiding light. Your unwavering support and love have shaped me into the person I am today.

Dad: While you were hard on us growing up, I appreciate the gifts I've gained from it: a strong work ethic, perseverance, grit, and profound compassion. You are my greatest teacher, and our bond is everything to me. Thank you for pushing me to be my best and for always believing in me.

Willy: I love you more than words can say. I'm proud of our family, of our relationship, and the way you've always followed your heart. Your courage and authenticity inspire me every day.

Ben: I love you, my brother. You still find ways to push my buttons, play with my spirit and put a smile on my face. You are with me always.

To my wife and my new family: I adore you. Your love and partnership have brought me immeasurable joy. **Leo**, you are my brightest inspiration. You teach me to be true to myself no matter what. Your presence in my life is a gift I cherish every day.

Jim and Sue: Thank you for welcoming me in a difficult time with such unconditional love. Your kindness and acceptance have meant the world to me.

Torey: Thank you for sticking with me when it got the messiest. I appreciate your forgiveness, your love, your truth, and your friendship. You are a soul sister, and I am grateful for the deep bond we share.

Stephen: Love you, butt face. Thank you for being such a wayshower and leader for me on this spiritual journey. Your wisdom and guidance have been invaluable.

To the United Methodist Church of Eagle Valley: A special thank you for trusting me, for opening your minds and hearts to a brand new pastor. Thank you for supporting me through the mess. Much love to you all.

To Alee and all at 10/10 Press: Thank you for helping me to find my voice, to move through when it's hard, and heal through writing. Your support and belief in me have been crucial to this journey.

To anyone struggling in the dark: It fucking sucks, I know. I know you feel alone. I hear your pain. I get the depths of it. I do this all for you to know you are not alone, you are so loved, and you are needed.

All my love, Molly

About the Author

From medical office administrator to suicide prevention trainer and United Methodist pastor, Molly Booker's life has always been about finding the soul line: the equilibrium of personal passion with the pursuit of aligned success.

As the executive director of SpeakUpReachOut, Molly channeled her personal struggles with suicidal ideation and depression into a passionate role leading programming and initiates across Colorado. As a peer specialist at Mind Springs, Molly was responsible for peer support services for clients with serious mental illnesses.

Molly's work in suicide prevention, paired with her own lived experience with mental health struggles, led her down a spiritual path that culminated in joining the United Methodist Church and becoming a pastor. Her soul searching continued, and when Molly met Kelly it became clear: Molly was not meant for her husband; Molly was meant for Kelly.

Now, Molly is a writer, speaker, and a passionate advocate for LGBTQ+ rights and suicide prevention.

www.ingramcontent.com/pod-product-compliance
Lightning Source LLC
Jackson TN
JSHW020142040125
76470JS00003B/17